On
Negotiation

HBR's 10 Must Reads series is the definitive collection of ideas and best practices for aspiring and experienced leaders alike. These books offer essential reading selected from the pages of *Harvard Business Review* on topics critical to the success of every manager.

Titles include:

HBR's 10 Must Reads 2015
HBR's 10 Must Reads 2016
HBR's 10 Must Reads 2017
HBR's 10 Must Reads 2018
HBR's 10 Must Reads 2019
HBR's 10 Must Reads 2020
HBR's 10 Must Reads for CEOs
HBR's 10 Must Reads for New Managers
HBR's 10 Must Reads on AI, Analytics, and the New Machine Age
HBR's 10 Must Reads on Business Model Innovation
HBR's 10 Must Reads on Change Management
HBR's 10 Must Reads on Collaboration
HBR's 10 Must Reads on Communication
HBR's 10 Must Reads on Diversity
HBR's 10 Must Reads on Emotional Intelligence
HBR's 10 Must Reads on Entrepreneurship and Startups
HBR's 10 Must Reads on Innovation
HBR's 10 Must Reads on Leadership
HBR's 10 Must Reads on Leadership for Healthcare
HBR's 10 Must Reads on Leadership Lessons from Sports
HBR's 10 Must Reads on Making Smart Decisions
HBR's 10 Must Reads on Managing Across Cultures
HBR's 10 Must Reads on Managing People
HBR's 10 Must Reads on Managing Yourself
HBR's 10 Must Reads on Mental Toughness
HBR's 10 Must Reads on Negotiation
HBR's 10 Must Reads on Nonprofits and the Social Sectors

On
Negotiation

HARVARD BUSINESS REVIEW PRESS
Boston, Massachusetts

Library of Congress Cataloging-in-Publication Data

Title: HBR's 10 must reads on negotiation.
Other titles: Harvard Business Review's ten must reads on negotiation | Negotiation | HBR's 10 must reads (Series)
Description: Boston, Massachusetts : Harvard Business Review Press, [2019] | Series: HBR's 10 must reads series | Includes index.
Identifiers: LCCN 2018057862 | ISBN 9781633697751 (pbk.)
Subjects: LCSH: Negotiation. | Negotiation in business.
Classification: LCC HD58.6 .H41 2019 | DDC 158/.5—dc23 LC record available at https://lccn.loc.gov/2018057862

ISBN: 978-1-63369-775-1
eISBN: 978-1-63369-776-8

The paper used in this publication meets the requirements of the American National Standard for Permanence of Paper for Publications and Documents in Libraries and Archives Z39.48-1992.

Contents

On
Negotiation

Six Habits of Merely Effective Negotiators

by James K. Sebenius

GLOBAL DEAL MAKERS did a staggering $3.3 trillion worth of M&A transactions in 1999—and that's only a fraction of the capital that passed through negotiators' hands that year. Behind the deal-driven headlines, executives endlessly negotiate with customers and suppliers, with large shareholders and creditors, with prospective joint venture and alliance partners, with people inside their companies and across national borders. Indeed, wherever parties with different interests and perceptions depend on each other for results, negotiation matters. Little wonder that Bob Davis, vice chairman of Terra Lycos, has said that companies "have to make deal making a core competency."

Luckily, whether from schoolbooks or the school of hard knocks, most executives know the basics of negotiation; some are spectacularly adept. Yet high stakes and intense pressure can result in costly mistakes. Bad habits creep in, and experience can further ingrain those habits. Indeed, when I reflect on the thousands of negotiations I have participated in and studied over the years, I'm struck by how frequently even experienced negotiators leave money on the table, deadlock, damage relationships, or allow conflict to spiral. (For more on the rich theoretical understanding of negotiations developed by researchers over the past fifty years, see the sidebar "Academics Take a Seat at the Negotiating Table.")

There are as many specific reasons for bad outcomes in negotiations as there are individuals and deals. Yet broad classes of errors recur. In this article, I'll explore those mistakes, comparing good negotiating practice with bad. But first, let's take a closer look at the right negotiation problem that your approach must solve.

Solving the Right Negotiation Problem

In any negotiation, each side ultimately must choose between two options: accepting a deal or taking its best no-deal option—that is, the course of action it would take if the deal were not possible. As a negotiator, you seek to advance the full set of your interests by persuading the other side to say yes—and mean it—to a proposal that meets your interests better than your best no-deal option does. And why should the other side say yes? Because the deal meets its own interests better than its best no-deal option. So, while protecting your own choice, your negotiation problem is to understand and shape your counterpart's perceived decision—deal versus no deal—so that the other side chooses *in its own interest* what you want. As Italian diplomat Daniele Vare said long ago about diplomacy, negotiation is "the art of letting them have your way."

This approach may seem on the surface like a recipe for manipulation. But in fact, understanding your counterpart's interests and shaping the decision so the other side agrees for its own reasons is the key to jointly creating and claiming sustainable value from a negotiation. Yet even experienced negotiators make six common mistakes that keep them from solving the right problem.

Mistake 1: Neglecting the Other Side's Problem

You can't negotiate effectively unless you understand your own interests and your own no-deal options. So far, so good—but there's much more to it than that. Since the other side will say yes for its reasons, not yours, agreement requires understanding and addressing your counterpart's problem as a means to solving your own.

Idea in Brief

High stakes. Intense pressure. Careless mistakes. These can turn your key negotiations into disasters. Even seasoned negotiators bungle deals, leaving money on the table and damaging working relationships.

Why? During negotiations, six common mistakes can distract you from your *real* purpose: getting the other guy to choose what you want—for *his* own reasons.

Avoid negotiation pitfalls by mastering the art of letting the other guy have your way—*everyone* will win.

At a minimum, you need to understand the problem from the other side's perspective. Consider a technology company, whose board of directors pressed hard to develop a hot new product shortly after it went public. The company had developed a technology for detecting leaks in underground gas tanks that was both cheaper and about 100 times more accurate than existing technologies—at a time when the Environmental Protection Agency was persuading Congress to mandate that these tanks be continuously tested. Not surprisingly, the directors thought their timing was perfect and pushed employees to commercialize and market the technology in time to meet the demand. To their dismay, the company's first sale turned out to be its only one. Quite a mystery, since the technology worked, the product was less expensive, and the regulations did come through. Imagine the sales engineers confidently negotiating with a customer for a new order: "This technology costs less and is more accurate than the competition's." Think for a moment, though, about how intended buyers might mull over their interests, especially given that EPA regulations permitted leaks of up to 1,500 gallons while the new technology could pick up an 8-ounce leak. Potential buyer: "What a technological tour de force! This handy new device will almost certainly get me into needless, expensive regulatory trouble. And create P.R. problems too. I think I'll pass, but my competition should definitely have it." From the technology company's perspective, "faster, better, cheaper" added up to a sure deal; to the other side, it looked like a headache. No deal.

Idea in Practice

Negotiation Mistakes

Neglecting the other side's problem. If you don't understand the deal from the other side's perspective, you can't solve his problem *or* yours.

Example: A technology company that created a cheap, accurate way of detecting gas-tank leaks couldn't sell its product. Why? EPA regulations permitted leaks of up to 1,500 gallons, while this new technology detected *8-ounce* leaks. Fearing the device would spawn regulatory trouble, potential customers said, "No deal!"

Letting price bulldoze other interests. Most deals involve interests *besides* price:

- a positive working relationship, crucial in longer-term deals
- the social contract, or "spirit of the deal," including goodwill and shared expectations

- the deal-making process—personal, respectful, and fair to both sides

Price-centric tactics leave these potential *joint* gains unrealized.

Letting positions drive out interests. Incompatible *positions* may mask compatible *interests*. Your gain isn't necessarily your "opponent's" loss.

Example: Environmentalists and farmers opposed a power company's proposed dam. Yet compatible *interests* underlay these seemingly irreconcilable positions: Farmers wanted water flow; environmentalists, wildlife protection; the power company, a greener image. By agreeing to a smaller dam, water-flow guarantees, and habitat conservation, everyone won.

Searching too hard for common ground. While common ground helps negotiations, *different*

Social psychologists have documented the difficulty most people have understanding the other side's perspective. From the trenches, successful negotiators concur that overcoming this self-centered tendency is critical. As Millennium Pharmaceuticals' Steve Holtzman put it after a string of deals vaulted his company from a startup in 1993 to a major player with a $10.6 billion market cap today, "We spend a lot of time thinking about how the poor guy or woman on the other side of the table is going to have to go sell this deal to his or her boss. We spend a lot of time trying to understand how they are modeling it."

interests can give each party what it values most, at minimum cost to the other.

Example: An acquirer and entrepreneur disagree on the entrepreneurial company's likely future. To satisfy their differing interests, the buyer agrees to pay a fixed amount now and contingent amount later, based on future performance. Both find the deal more attractive than walking away.

Neglecting BATNA. BATNAs ("best alternative to a negotiated agreement") represent your actions if the proposed deal weren't possible; e.g., walk away, approach another buyer. Assessing your own *and* your partner's BATNA reveals surprising possibilities.

Example: A company hoping to sell a struggling division for somewhat more than its $7 million value had two fiercely competitive bidders.

Speculating each might pay an inflated price to trump the other, the seller ensured each knew its rival was looking. The division's selling price? *$45 million.*

Failing to correct for skewed vision. Two forms of bias can prompt errors:

- *Role bias*—overcommitting to your own point of view and interpreting information in self-serving ways. A plaintiff believes he has a 70% chance of winning his case, while the defense puts the odds at 50%. Result? Unlikelihood of out-of-court settlement.

- *Partisan perceptions*—painting your side with positive qualities, while vilifying your "opponent." Self-fulfilling prophecies may result.

Counteract these biases with role-plays of the opposition's interests.

And Wayne Huizenga, veteran of more than a thousand deals building Waste Management, AutoNation, and Blockbuster, distilled his extensive experience into basic advice that is often heard but even more often forgotten. "In all my years of doing deals, a few rules and lessons have emerged. Most important, always try to put yourself in the other person's shoes. It's vital to try to understand in depth what the other side really wants out of the deal."

Tough negotiators sometimes see the other side's concerns but dismiss them: "That's their problem and their issue. Let them handle it. We'll look after our own problems." This attitude can undercut your ability to profitably influence how your counterpart sees its problem. Early in his deal-making career at Cisco Systems, Mike Volpi, now chief strategy officer, had trouble completing proposed deals, his "outward confidence" often mistaken for arrogance. Many acquisitions later, a colleague observed that "the most important part of [Volpi's] development is that he learned power doesn't come from telling people you are powerful. He went from being a guy driving the deal from his side of the table to the guy who understood the deal from the other side."

An associate of Rupert Murdoch remarked that, as a buyer, Murdoch "understands the seller—and, whatever the guy's trying to do, he crafts his offer that way." If you want to change someone's mind, you should first learn where that person's mind is. Then, together, you can try to build what my colleague Bill Ury calls a "golden bridge," spanning the gulf between where your counterpart is now and your desired end point. This is much more effective than trying to shove the other side from its position to yours. As an eighteenth-century pope once noted about Cardinal de Polignac's remarkable diplomatic skills, "This young man always seems to be of my opinion [at the start of a negotiation], and at the end of the conversation I find that I am of his." In short, the first mistake is to focus on your own problem, exclusively. Solve the other side's as the means to solving your own.

Mistake 2: Letting Price Bulldoze Other Interests

Negotiators who pay attention exclusively to price turn potentially cooperative deals into adversarial ones. These "reverse Midas" negotiators, as I like to call them, use hard-bargaining tactics that often leave potential joint gains unrealized. That's because, while price is an important factor in most deals, it's rarely the only one. As Felix Rohatyn, former managing partner of the investment bank Lazard Frères, observed, "Most deals are 50% emotion and 50% economics."

There's a large body of research to support Rohatyn's view. Consider, for example, a simplified negotiation, extensively studied in

Academics Take a Seat
at the Negotiating Table

PARALLELING THE GROWTH in real-world negotiation, several genera-
tions of researchers have deepened our understanding of the process. In the
1950s and 1960s, elements of hard (win-lose) bargaining were isolated and
refined: how to set aggressive targets, start high, concede slowly, and employ
threats, bluffs, and commitments to positions without triggering an impasse
or escalation. By the early 1980s, with the win-win revolution popularized by
the book *Getting to Yes* (by Roger Fisher, William Ury, and Bruce Patton), the
focus shifted from battling over the division of the pie to the means of expanding it by uncovering and reconciling underlying interests. More sophisticated
analysis in Howard Raiffa's *Art and Science of Negotiation* soon transcended
this simplistic "win-win versus win-lose" debate; the pie obviously had to
be both expanded and divided. In *The Manager as Negotiator* (by David Lax
and James Sebenius), new guidance emerged on productively managing the
tension between the cooperative moves necessary to create value and the
competitive moves involved in claiming it. As the 1990s progressed with work
such as *Negotiating Rationally* (by Max Bazerman and Margaret Neale), the
behavioral study of negotiation—describing how people actually negotiate—
began to merge with the game theoretic approach, which prescribed how
fully rational people should negotiate. This new synthesis—developing the
best possible advice without assuming strictly rational behavior—is producing rich insights in negotiations ranging from simple two-party, one-shot,
single-issue situations through complex coalitional dealings over multiple
issues over time, where internal negotiations must be synchronized with external ones. Negotiation courses that explore these ideas have always been
popular options at business schools, but reflecting the growing recognition
of their importance, these courses are beginning to be required as part of
MBA core programs at schools such as Harvard. Rather than a special skill for
making major deals or resolving disputes, negotiation has become a way of
life for effective executives.

---

academic labs, involving real money. One party is given, say, $100 to
divide with another party as she likes; the second party can agree or
disagree to the arrangement. If he agrees, the $100 is divided in line
with the first side's proposal; if not, neither party gets anything. A
pure price logic would suggest proposing something like $99 for me,
$1 for you. Although this is an extreme allocation, it still represents
a position in which your counterpart gets something rather than

nothing. Pure price negotiators confidently predict the other side will agree to the split; after all, they've been offered free money—it's like finding a dollar on the street and putting it in your pocket. Who wouldn't pick it up?

In reality, however, most players turn down proposals that don't let them share in at least 35% to 40% of the bounty—even when much larger stakes are involved and the amount they forfeit is significant. While these rejections are "irrational" on a pure price basis and virtually incomprehensible to reverse Midas types, studies show that when a split feels too unequal to people, they reject the spoils as unfair, are offended by the process, and perhaps try to teach the "greedy" person a lesson.

An important real-world message is embedded in these lab results: people care about much more than the absolute level of their own economic outcome; competing interests include relative results, perceived fairness, self-image, reputation, and so on. Successful negotiators, acknowledging that economics aren't everything, focus on four important nonprice factors.

The relationship

Less experienced negotiators often undervalue the importance of developing working relationships with the other parties, putting the relationships at risk by overly tough tactics or simple neglect. This is especially true in cross-border deals. In much of Latin America, southern Europe, and Southeast Asia, for example, relationships—rather than transactions—can be the predominant negotiating interest when working out longer-term deals. Results-oriented North Americans, Northern Europeans, and Australians often come to grief by underestimating the strength of this interest and insisting prematurely that the negotiators "get down to business."

The social contract

Similarly, negotiators tend to focus on the economic contract—equity splits, cost sharing, governance, and so on—at the expense of the social contract, or the "spirit of a deal." Going well beyond a good working relationship, the social contract governs people's expectations about the nature, extent, and duration of the venture, about process, and about the way unforeseen events will be handled. Especially in new ventures and strategic alliances, where goodwill and strong shared expectations are extremely important, negotiating a positive social contract is an important way to reinforce economic contracts. Scurrying to check founding documents when conflicts occur, which they inevitably do, can signal a badly negotiated social contract.

The process
Negotiators often forget that the deal-making process can be as important as its content. The story is told of the young Tip O'Neill, who later became Speaker of the House, meeting an elderly constituent on the streets of his North Cambridge, Massachusetts, district. Surprised to learn that she was not planning to vote for him, O'Neill probed, "Haven't you known me and my family all my life?" "Yes." "Haven't I cut your grass in summer and shoveled your walk in winter?" "Yes." "Don't you agree with all my policies and positions?" "Yes." "Then why aren't you going to vote for me?" "Because you didn't ask me to." Considerable academic research confirms what O'Neill learned from this conversation: process counts. What's more, sustainable results are more often reached when all parties perceive the process as personal, respectful, straightforward, and fair.[1]

The interests of the full set of players
Less experienced negotiators sometimes become mesmerized by the aggregate economics of a deal and forget about the interests of players who are in a position to torpedo it. When the boards of pharmaceutical giants Glaxo and SmithKline Beecham publicly announced their merger in 1998, investors were thrilled, rapidly *increasing* the combined company's market capitalization by a stunning $20 billion. Yet despite prior agreement on who would occupy which top executive positions in the newly combined company, internal disagreement about management control and position resurfaced and sank the announced deal, and the $20 billion evaporated. (Overwhelming strategic logic ultimately drove the

companies back together, but only after nearly two years had passed.) This episode confirms two related lessons. First, while favorable overall economics are generally necessary, they are often not sufficient. Second, keep all potentially influential internal players on your radar screen; don't lose sight of their interests or their capacity to affect the deal. What is "rational" for the whole may not be so for the parts.

It can be devilishly difficult to cure the reverse Midas touch. If you treat a potentially cooperative negotiation like a pure price deal, it will likely become one. Imagine a negotiator who expects a hard-ball, price-driven process. She initiates the bid by taking a tough pre-emptive position; the other side is likely to reciprocate. "Aha!" says the negotiator, her suspicions confirmed. "I *knew* this was just going to be a tough price deal."

A negotiator can often influence whether price will dominate or be kept in perspective. Consider negotiations between two companies trying to establish an equity joint venture. Among other issues, they are trying to place a value on each side's contribution to determine ownership shares. A negotiator might drive this process down two very different paths. A price-focused approach quickly isolates the valuation issue and then bangs out a resolution. Alternatively, the two sides could first flesh out a more specific shared vision for the joint venture (together envisioning the "pot of gold" they could create), probe to understand the most critical concerns of each side—including price—and craft trade-offs among the full set of issues to meet these interests. In the latter approach, price becomes a component or even an implication of a larger, longer-term package, rather than the primary focus.

Some negotiations are indeed pure price deals and only about aggregate economics, but there is often much more to work with. Wise negotiators put the vital issue of price in perspective and don't straitjacket their view of the richer interests at stake. They work with the subjective as well as the objective, with the process and the relationship, with the "social contract" or spirit of a deal as well as its letter, and with the interests of the parts as well as the whole.

Mistake 3: Letting Positions Drive Out Interests

Three elements are at play in a negotiation. *Issues* are on the table for explicit agreement. *Positions* are one party's stands on the issues. *Interests* are underlying concerns that would be affected by the resolution. Of course, positions on issues reflect underlying interests, but they need not be identical. Suppose you're considering a job offer. The base salary will probably be an issue. Perhaps your position on that issue is that you need to earn $100,000. The interests underlying that position include your need for a good income but may also include status, security, new opportunities, and needs that can be met in ways other than salary. Yet even very experienced deal makers may see the essence of negotiation as a dance of positions. If incompatible positions finally converge, a deal is struck; if not, the negotiation ends in an impasse. By contrast, interest-driven bargainers see the process primarily as a reconciliation of underlying interests: you have one set of interests, I have another, and through joint problem solving we should be better able to meet both sets of interests and thus create new value.

Consider a dispute over a dam project. Environmentalists and farmers opposed a U.S. power company's plans to build a dam. The two sides had irreconcilable positions: "absolutely yes" and "no way." Yet these incompatible positions masked compatible interests. The farmers were worried about reduced water flow below the dam, the environmentalists were focused on the downstream habitat of the endangered whooping crane, and the power company needed new capacity and a greener image. After a costly legal stalemate, the three groups devised an interest-driven agreement that all of them considered preferable to continued court warfare. The agreement included a smaller dam built on a fast track, water flow guarantees, downstream habitat protection, and a trust fund to enhance whooping crane habitats elsewhere.

Despite the clear advantages of reconciling deeper interests, people have a built-in bias toward focusing on their own positions instead. This hardwired assumption that our interests are incompatible implies a zero-sum pie in which my gain is your loss. Research in psychology supports the mythical fixed-pie view as the norm. In a survey of 5,000 subjects in 32 negotiating studies, mostly carried out with monetary stakes, participants failed to realize compatible issues fully half of the time.[2] In real-world terms, this means that enormous value is unknowingly left uncreated as both sides walk away from money on the table.

Reverse Midas negotiators, for example, almost automatically fixate on price and bargaining positions to claim value. After the usual preliminaries, countless negotiations get serious when one side asks, "So, what's your position?" or says, "Here's my position." This positional approach often drives the process toward a ritual value-claiming dance. Great negotiators understand that the dance of bargaining positions is only the surface game; the real action takes place when they've probed behind positions for the full set of interests at stake. Reconciling interests to create value requires patience and a willingness to research the other side, ask many questions, and listen. It would be silly to write off either price or bargaining position; both are extremely important. And there is, of course, a limit to joint value creation. The trick is to recognize and productively manage the tension between cooperative actions needed to create value and competitive ones needed to claim it. The pie must be both expanded and divided.

Mistake 4: Searching Too Hard for Common Ground

Conventional wisdom says we negotiate to overcome the differences that divide us. So, typically, we're advised to find win-win agreements by searching for common ground. Common ground is generally a good thing. Yet many of the most frequently overlooked sources of value in negotiation arise from differences among the parties.

Recall the battle over the dam. The solution—a smaller dam, water flow guarantees, habitat conservation—did not result from common interests but because farmers, environmentalists, and the utility had different priorities. Similarly, when Egypt and Israel were negotiating over the Sinai, their positions on where to draw the boundary were incompatible. When negotiators went beyond the opposing positions, however, they uncovered a vital difference of underlying interest and priority: the Israelis cared more about security, while the Egyptians cared more about sovereignty. The solution was a demilitarized zone under the Egyptian flag. Differences of interest or priority can open the door to unbundling different elements and giving each party what it values the most—at the least cost to the other.

Even when an issue seems purely economic, finding differences can break open deadlocked deals. Consider a small technology company and its investors, stuck in a tough negotiation with a large strategic acquirer adamant about paying much less than the asking price. On investigation, it turned out that the acquirer was actually willing to pay the higher price but was concerned about raising price expectations in a fast-moving sector in which it planned to make more acquisitions. The solution was for the two sides to agree on a modest, well-publicized initial cash purchase price; the deal included complex-sounding contingencies that virtually guaranteed a much higher price later.

Differences in forecasts can also fuel joint gains. Suppose an entrepreneur who is genuinely optimistic about the prospects of her fast-growing company faces a potential buyer who likes the company but is much more skeptical about the company's future cash flow. They have negotiated in good faith, but, at the end of the day, the two sides sharply disagree on the likely future of the company and so cannot find an acceptable sale price. Instead of seeing these different forecasts as a barrier, a savvy negotiator could use them to bridge the value gap by proposing a deal in which the buyer pays a fixed amount now and a contingent amount later on the basis of the company's future performance. Properly structured with adequate incentives and monitoring mechanisms, such a contingent payment, or "earn-out," can appear quite valuable to the optimistic seller— who expects to get her higher valuation—but not very costly to the less optimistic buyer. And willingness to accept such a contingent deal may signal that the seller's confidence in the business is genuine. Both may find the deal much more attractive than walking away.

A host of other differences make up the raw material for joint gains. A less risk-averse party can "insure" a more risk-averse one. An impatient party can get most of the early money, while his more patient counterpart can get considerably more over a longer period of time. Differences in cost or revenue structure, tax status, or regulatory arrangements between two parties can be converted into gains for both. Indeed, conducting a disciplined "differences inventory" is at least as important a task as is identifying areas of common ground. After all, if we were all clones of one another, with the same interests, beliefs, attitudes toward risk and time, assets, and so on, there would be little to negotiate. While common ground helps, differences drive deals. But negotiators who don't actively search for differences rarely find them.

Mistake 5: Neglecting BATNAs

BATNAs—the acronym for "best alternative to a negotiated agreement" coined years ago by Roger Fisher, Bill Ury, and Bruce Patton in their book *Getting to Yes*—reflect the course of action a party would take if the proposed deal were not possible. A BATNA may involve walking away, prolonging a stalemate, approaching another potential buyer, making something in-house rather than procuring it externally, going to court rather than settling, forming a different alliance, or going on strike. BATNAs set the threshold—in terms of the full set of interests—that any acceptable agreement must exceed. Both parties doing better than their BATNAs is a necessary condition for an agreement. Thus BATNAs define a zone of possible agreement and determine its location.

A strong BATNA is an important negotiation tool. Many people associate the ability to inflict or withstand damage with bargaining power, but your willingness to walk away to an apparently good BATNA is often more important. The better your BATNA appears both to you and to the other party, the more credible your threat to walk away becomes, and the more it can serve as leverage to improve the deal. Roger Fisher has dramatized this point by asking which you would prefer to have in your back pocket during a compensation negotiation with your boss: a gun or a terrific job offer from a desirable employer who is also a serious competitor of your company?

Not only should you assess your own BATNA, you should also think carefully about the other side's. Doing so can alert you to surprising possibilities. In one instance, a British company hoped to sell a poorly performing division for a bit more than its depreciated asset value of $7 million to one of two potential buyers. Realizing that these buyers were fierce rivals in other markets, the seller speculated that each party might be willing to pay an inflated price to keep the other from getting the division. So they made sure that each suitor knew the other was looking and skillfully cultivated the interest of both companies. The division sold for $45 million.

Negotiators must also be careful not to inadvertently damage their BATNAs. I saw that happen at a Canadian chemical manufacturing company that had decided to sell a large but nonstrategic division to raise urgently needed cash. The CEO charged his second-in-command with negotiating the sale of the division at the highest possible price.

The target buyer was an Australian company, whose chief executive was an old school friend of the Canadian CEO. The Australian chief executive let it be known that his company was interested in the deal but that his senior management was consumed, at the moment, with other priorities. If the Australian company could have a nine-month negotiating exclusive to "confirm their seriousness about the sale," the Australian chief executive would dedicate the top personnel to make the deal happen. A chief-to-chief agreement to that effect was struck. Pity the second-in-command, charged with urgently maximizing cash from this sale, as he jetted off to Sydney with no meaningful alternative for nine endless months to whatever price the Australians offered.

Negotiators often become preoccupied with tactics, trying to improve the potential deal while neglecting their own BATNA and that of the other side. Yet the real negotiation problem is "deal versus BATNA," not one or the other in isolation. Your potential deal and

Solving Teddy Roosevelt's Negotiation Problem

THEODORE ROOSEVELT, nearing the end of a hard-fought presidential election campaign in 1912, scheduled a final whistle-stop journey. At each stop, Roosevelt planned to clinch the crowd's votes by distributing an elegant pamphlet with a stern presidential portrait on the cover and a stirring speech, "Confession of Faith," inside. Some 3 million copies had been printed when a campaign worker noticed a small line under the photograph on each brochure that read, "Moffett Studios, Chicago." Since Moffett held the copyright, the unauthorized use of the photo could cost the campaign one dollar per reproduction. With no time to reprint the brochure, what was the campaign to do?

Not using the pamphlets at all would damage Roosevelt's election prospects. Yet, if they went ahead, a scandal could easily erupt very close to the election, and the campaign could be liable for an unaffordable sum. Campaign workers quickly realized they would have to negotiate with Moffett. But research by their Chicago operatives turned up bad news: although early in his career as a photographer, Moffett had been taken with the potential of this new artistic medium, he had received little recognition. Now, Moffett was financially hard up and bitterly approaching retirement with a single-minded focus on money.

Dispirited, the campaign workers approached campaign manager George Perkins, a former partner of J.P. Morgan. Perkins lost no time summoning his stenographer to dispatch the following cable to Moffett Studios: "We are planning to distribute millions of pamphlets with Roosevelt's picture on the cover. It will be great publicity for the studio whose photograph we use. How much will you pay us to use yours? Respond immediately." Shortly, Moffett replied: "We've never done this before, but under the circumstances we'd be pleased to offer you $250." Reportedly, Perkins accepted—without dickering for more.

Perkins's misleading approach raises ethical yellow flags and is anything but a model negotiation on how to enhance working relationships. Yet this case

---

your BATNA should work together as the two blades of the scissors do to cut a piece of paper.

Mistake 6: Failing to Correct for Skewed Vision

You may be crystal clear on the right negotiation problem—but you can't solve it correctly without a firm understanding of both sides' interests, BATNAs, valuations, likely actions, and so on. Yet,

raises a very interesting question: why did the campaign workers find the prospect of this negotiation so difficult? Their inability to see what Perkins immediately perceived flowed from their anxious obsession with their own side's problem: their blunders so far, the high risk of losing the election, a potential $3 million exposure, an urgent deadline, and no cash to meet Moffett's likely demands for something the campaign vitally needed. Had they avoided mistake 1 by pausing for a moment and thinking about how Moffett saw his problem, they would have realized that Moffett didn't even know he had a problem. Perkins's tactical genius was to recognize the essence of the negotiator's central task: shape how your counterpart sees its problem such that it chooses what you want.

The campaign workers were paralyzed in the face of what they saw as sharply conflicting monetary interests and their pathetic BATNA. From their perspective, Moffett's only choice was how to exploit their desperation at the prospect of losing the presidency. By contrast, dodging mistake 5, Perkins immediately grasped the importance of favorably shaping Moffett's BATNA perceptions, both of the campaign's (awful) no-deal options and Moffett's (powerful) one. Perkins looked beyond price, positions, and common ground (mistakes 2, 3, and 4) and used Moffett's different interests to frame the photographer's choice as "the value of publicity and recognition." Had he assumed this would be a standard, hardball price deal by offering a small amount to start, not only would this assumption have been dead wrong but, worse, it would have been self-fulfilling.

Risky and ethically problematic? Yes . . . but Perkins saw his options as certain disaster versus some chance of avoiding it. And was Moffett really entitled to a $3 million windfall, avoidable had the campaign caught its oversight a week beforehand? Hard to say, but this historical footnote, which I've greatly embellished, illuminates the intersection of negotiating mistakes, tactics, and ethics.

just as a pilot's sense of the horizon at night or in a storm can be wildly inaccurate, the psychology of perception systematically leads negotiators to major errors.[3]

Self-serving role bias

People tend unconsciously to interpret information pertaining to their own side in a strongly self-serving way. The following experiment shows the process at work. Harvard researchers gave a large group of executives financial and industry information about one company negotiating to acquire another. The executive subjects were randomly assigned to the negotiating roles of buyer or seller; the information provided to each side was identical. After plenty of time for analysis, all subjects were asked for their private assessment of the target company's fair value—as distinct from how they might portray that value in the bargaining process. Those assigned the role of seller gave median valuations more than twice those given by the executives assigned to the buyer's role. These valuation gulfs had no basis in fact; they were driven entirely by random role assignments.

Even comparatively modest role biases can blow up potential deals. Suppose a plaintiff believes he has a 70% chance of winning a million-dollar judgment, while the defense thinks the plaintiff has only a 50% chance of winning. This means that, in settlement talks, the plaintiff's expected BATNA for a court battle (to get $700,000 minus legal fees) will exceed the defendant's assessment of his exposure (to pay $500,000 plus fees). Without significant risk aversion, the divergent assessments would block any out-of-court settlement. This cognitive role bias helps explain why Microsoft took such a confrontational approach in its recent struggle with the U.S. Department of Justice. The company certainly appeared overoptimistic about its chances in court. Similarly, Arthur Andersen likely exhibited overconfidence in its arbitration prospects over the terms of separation from Andersen Consulting (now Accenture). Getting too committed to your point of view—"believing your own line"—is an extremely common mistake.

Partisan perceptions

While we systematically err in processing information critical to our own side, we are even worse at assessing the other side—especially in an adversarial situation. Extensive research has documented an unconscious mechanism that enhances one's own side, "portraying it as more talented, honest, and morally upright," while simultaneously vilifying the opposition. This often leads to exaggerated perceptions of the other side's position and overestimates of the actual substantive conflict. To an outsider, those caught up in disintegrating partnerships or marriages often appear to hold exaggerated views of each other. Such partisan perceptions can become even more virulent among people on each side of divides, such as Israelis and Palestinians, Bosnian Muslims and the Serbs, or Catholics and Protestants in Northern Ireland.

Partisan perceptions can easily become self-fulfilling prophecies. Experiments testing the effects of teachers' expectations of students, psychiatrists' diagnoses of mental patients, and platoon leaders' expectations of their trainees confirm the notion that partisan perceptions often shape behavior. At the negotiating table, clinging firmly to the idea that one's counterpart is stubborn or extreme, for example, is likely to trigger just that behavior, sharply reducing the possibility of reaching a constructive agreement.

As disagreement and conflict intensify, sophisticated negotiators should expect biased perceptions, both on their own side and the other side. Less seasoned players tend to be shocked and outraged by perceived extremism and are wholly unaware that their own views are likely colored by their roles. How to counteract these powerful biases? Just knowing that they exist helps. Seeking the views of outside, uninvolved parties is useful, too. And having people on your side prepare the strongest possible case for the other side can serve as the basis for preparatory role-playing that can generate valuable insights. A few years ago, helping a client get ready for a tough deal, I suggested that the client create a detailed "brief" for each side and have the team's best people negotiate for the other side in a reverse role-play. The brief for my client's side was lengthy, eloquent, and persuasive. Tellingly, the brief describing the other side's situation was only two pages long and consisted mainly of reasons for conceding quickly to my client's superior arguments. Not only were my client's executives fixated on their own problem (mistake 1), their perceptions of each side were also hopelessly biased (mistake 6). To prepare effectively, they needed to undertake significant competitive research and reality-test their views with uninvolved outsiders.

From Merely Effective to Superior Negotiation

So you have navigated the shoals of merely effective deal making to face what is truly the right problem. You have focused on the full set of interests of all parties, rather than fixating on price and positions. You have looked beyond common ground to unearth value-creating differences. You have assessed and shaped BATNAs. You have taken steps to avoid role biases and partisan perceptions. In short, you have grasped your own problem clearly and have sought to understand and influence the other side's such that what it chooses is what you want.

Plenty of errors still lie in wait: cultural gaffes, an irritating style, inadvertent signals of disrespect or untrustworthiness, miscommunication, bad timing, revealing too much or too little, a poorly designed agenda, mistakes, negotiating with the wrong person on the other side, personalizing issues, and so on. Even if you manage to avoid these mistakes as well, you may still run into difficulties by approaching the negotiation far too narrowly, taking too many of the elements of the "problem" as fixed.

The very best negotiators take a broader approach to setting up and solving the right problem. With a keen sense of the potential value to be created as their guiding beacon, these negotiators are game-changing entrepreneurs. They envision the most promising architecture and take action to bring it into being. These virtuoso negotiators not only play the game as given at the table, they are masters at setting it up and changing it away from the table to maximize the chances for better results.

To advance the full set of their interests, they understand and shape the other side's choice—deal versus no deal—such that the other chooses what they want. As François de Callières, an eighteenth-century commentator, once put it, negotiation masters possess "the supreme art of making every man offer him as a gift that which it was his chief design to secure."

Originally published in April 2001. Reprint R0104E

Notes

1. W. Chan Kim and Renée Mauborgne, "Fair Process: Managing in the Knowledge Economy," HBR July–August 1997.

2. This and other studies illustrating this point can be found in Leigh Thompson's *The Mind and Heart of the Negotiator* (Upper Saddle River, NJ: Prentice Hall, 1998).

3. See Robert J. Robinson, "Errors in Social Judgment: Implications for Negotiation and Conflict Resolution, Part I: Biased Assimilation of Information," Harvard Business School, 1997, and Robert J. Robinson, "Errors in Social Judgment: Implications for Negotiation and Conflict Resolution, Part II: Partisan Perceptions," Harvard Business School, 1997.

Control the Negotiation Before It Begins

by Deepak Malhotra

COUNTLESS BOOKS and articles offer advice that can help deal makers avoid missteps at the bargaining table. But some of the costliest mistakes take place before negotiators even sit down to discuss the substance of the deal. That's because people fall prey to a seemingly reasonable—but ultimately faulty—assumption about deal making. Negotiators often take it for granted that if they bring a lot of value to the table and have sufficient leverage, they'll be able to strike a great deal. While those things are certainly important, many other factors influence where each party ends up.

In this article I draw on my experience advising scores of companies on deals worth millions or billions of dollars to present four factors that can have a tremendous impact on negotiation outcomes. In each case, I provide guidance on what negotiators should do before either side starts making offers or counteroffers.

1. Negotiate Process Before Substance

A couple of years ago, two cofounders of a tech venture walked into a meeting with the CEO of a *Fortune* 100 company who had agreed to invest $10 million with them. A week earlier, the parties had hammered out the investment amount and valuation, so the meeting was supposed to be celebratory more than anything else. When the cofounders entered the room, they were surprised to see a team of lawyers and bankers. The CEO was also there, but it soon became clear that he was not going to actively participate.

As soon as the cofounders sat down, the bankers on the other side started to renegotiate the deal. The $10 million investment was still on the table, but now they demanded a much lower valuation; in other words, the cofounders would have to give up significantly more equity. Their attempts to explain that an agreement had already been reached were to no avail.

What was going on? Had the cofounders misunderstood the level of commitment in the previous meeting? Had they overlooked steps involved in finalizing the deal? Had the CEO intended to renege all along—or had his team convinced him that the deal could be sweetened?

Upset and confused, the cofounders quickly assessed their options. Accepting the new deal would hurt financially (and psychologically), but they'd get the $10 million in needed funds. On the other hand, doing so would significantly undervalue what they brought to the table. They decided to walk out without a deal. Before they left, they emphasized their strong desire to do a deal on the initial terms and explained that this was a matter of principle as well as economics. Within hours, they were on a plane, not knowing what would happen. A few days later, the CEO called and accepted the original deal.

The gutsy move worked out for the cofounders, but it would have been better not to let things go wrong in the first place. Their mistake was a common one: focusing too much on the substance of the deal and not enough on the process. Substance is the terms that make up the final agreement. Process is how you will get from where you are today to that agreement. My advice to deal makers: Negotiate process before substance.

Consider another scenario. You've been negotiating with someone for months. You have a few final concessions that you've been holding back—they're costly but worth making if it will close the deal. With the finish line in sight, you make the concessions, and

Idea in Brief

The Problem

Some of the costliest mistakes in negotiations take place *before* anyone sits down at the bargaining table. That's because deal makers tend to focus too much on substance—offers, counteroffers, concessions—and not enough on process.

The Solution

Four strategies can help set the stage for a successful negotiation.

- Negotiators need to address matters of process at the outset.

- They must set realistic expectations.

- They need to clearly identify all players that will influence or be influenced by the deal.

- And they must set the psychological frame through which the deal will be viewed.

the other side responds: "This is great. I appreciate your flexibility on these issues. Let me share this with my boss to see what she thinks." Unfortunately for you, you had no idea your counterpart even had a boss—you thought he was the final decision maker. The negotiations are clearly not over, and you have nothing left to give.

The more clarity and commitment you have regarding the process, the less likely you are to make mistakes on substance. Negotiating process entails discussing and influencing a range of factors that will affect the outcome of the deal. Ask the other party: How much time does your company need to close the deal? Who must be on board? What factors might slow down or speed up the process? Are there key milestones or dates we should be aware of? Remember to find out simple things such as, Who will be in the meeting tomorrow? What will the agenda be? Since we are not going to discuss the issues of importance to us in the next meeting, when will we address them?

Of course, you can't always get clear answers to every question at the outset—and sometimes it is premature to ask certain questions. But you should seek to clarify and reach agreement on as many process elements as possible—and as early as is appropriate—to avoid stumbling on substance later.

2. Normalize the Process

A businessman who owns multiple manufacturing facilities in Asia once told me that he no longer does business with companies from the West unless their top managers are willing to first fly into his city to meet with him. My initial thoughts were: Is this about ego? Is it about building relationships? Is it a cultural norm or ritual of some sort? Actually, none of those had anything to do with his precondition to signing a contract.

Here's how he explained it to me: "Until they have flown into my city and then driven to our manufacturing plants—which are located 20 kilometers from the airport but take almost three hours to reach—until they have experienced that, they simply don't understand how things work around here. And if they don't understand, we run into serious problems. Because the first time there is a delay or disruption, or if we need to renegotiate something, they will immediately assume we are either incompetent or stealing from them. Once they've seen how things actually work, we can have a more productive relationship."

Unless business partners understand what is "normal" in a given context or culture, they are likely to misunderstand or overreact to adverse events. The same is true in negotiations of all kinds: It is important to normalize the process. If you've ever been involved in an ugly conflict that went into mediation, you may have seen this in action. When a good mediator sits down with parties who are in a bitter dispute, she might say something like, "You think you hate each other today? I can assure you, about three days into this process, you're going to hate each other even more. And when that happens, I want you to remember something: That's normal."

If the mediator does not give this warning, the parties are much more likely to abandon the process when emotions heighten and things seem to be falling apart. But if she explains at the outset that it's normal for things to get worse before they get better, the parties are more likely to keep at it. By normalizing the process, she effectively manages their expectations.

The same principle applies to any negotiation where there's a risk that things will not go perfectly smoothly. If you anticipate delays or disruptions on your side, tell your counterparts. This allows you to shape how they will interpret a negative event should one occur and to ensure that they do not overweight its significance. You'll have a much harder time trying to influence their perceptions or win back their trust after something goes wrong that they did not expect.

Normalizing the process entails discussing, in advance, any factors that might cause the other side to question your intentions or ability or to doubt the likelihood of a successful outcome. You might explain typical barriers that need to be overcome, moments during the process when it's common for parties to feel anxious or pessimistic, events that might delay progress, and the difference between disruptions that are commonplace and easy to resolve and ones that are more serious.

Encourage the other side to do the same for you. People often hesitate to discuss "what might go wrong," because they're focused on presenting themselves and the merits of the deal in the best possible light. This is especially true in certain cultures and in contexts where competition is fierce. Your counterpart might be thinking, "Why should I talk about problems if my rivals are pretending things will be great?"

That's understandable. If other parties think that mentioning a potential disruption could cost them the business, or that you'll use it as a lever to extract greater concessions, they're unlikely to be truthful. To encourage people to be open about problems, make it safe for them. Explain that you are experienced enough to know that every deal and relationship is likely to encounter difficulties and disruptions, and that you want to learn more about the specific risk factors that might play a role in this case. And if you can signal (or commit to) having no intention of holding those factors against them, you have a better chance of reaching an understanding that works for both sides.

3. Map Out the Negotiation Space

Some years ago, a client of mine was preparing to sell his stake in a company that was jointly owned by four entities. The owners had been squabbling for many years; it was clear that the asset would need to be consolidated under one party (or perhaps two who could get along). It was also clear that no one wanted to sell. However, there was little choice in the matter, because one of the owners—Company X—was a much larger company with the power and the clout to push people out. It announced that it would buy out the other three.

My client wanted to wait until Company X had bought out the other two owners before negotiating the sale of his shares. He figured that by being "the last piece of the puzzle," he would be able to hold out for more money.

When we met to discuss his strategy, I asked him to step back and "map out the negotiation space." This consists of every party that can affect the negotiation, along with any party that will be affected by the negotiation. In my experience, a strategy that makes perfect sense when you're thinking bilaterally—that is, about the relationship between any two parties in the negotiation—can suddenly become ineffective or even disastrous when you take a multilateral perspective. I encouraged my client to evaluate the interests, constraints, alternatives, and perspective of all the relevant parties. One of the things we looked at was how much equity each party had and how much of the board each one controlled:

The negotiation space

COMPANY X
1/3 of shares
2 board seats

↕

COMPANY A	CLIENT	COMPANY B
1/3 of shares	1/6 of shares	1/6 of shares
2 board seats	1 board seat	0 board seats

We then focused on the interests of each company: What exactly are their interests in this deal? How would you rank their priorities? The four parties had known one another a long time, and my client did not have any trouble identifying what mattered most to each. Company X, for example, was concerned about three things, and its priorities were as follows: (1) Reputation: It did not want ties with any organization that could hurt its reputation. (2) Control: It wanted ownership only in businesses where it had a majority of board seats. (3) Money: It would want to pay as little as possible, but this was not as big a concern as reputation and control.

After delving into the perspectives of all parties, we unearthed one more important bit of information: Company A was the least interested in selling and was already putting up a fight that could drag things out.

When we put all these details together, it became clear that the "last piece of the puzzle" strategy would be unwise. Why?

For Company X, control was a higher priority than money. To get control, it needed to buy either my client or Company A—as soon as it made either purchase, it would control more than 50% of the board seats and hence the company (for most decisions). Therefore, if my client were the last to sell, he would be negotiating with Company X after it had control. At that time, my client would be able to get paid only for his 1/6 share of the firm's equity. But if he were to sell first, at a time when Company A was refusing to sell and was making things difficult for Company X, he could monetize two assets: his shares and his board seat. In other words, the last party to negotiate would have the least leverage and limited opportunities to monetize its assets.

In the real world, you'll never have as complete a picture as you'd like, but you put yourself at further disadvantage if you focus too narrowly on the party on the other side of the table. You have to assess the perspective of all the parties that can influence or are influenced by the deal: Who has the ability to influence the person on the other side of the table? How might the strategy or actions of other parties change your alternatives, for better or worse? How does the deal affect the interests of those who are *not* at the table? How will this negotiation affect your leverage with future negotiation partners? If multiple parties are involved in the deal, does it make sense to negotiate with them simultaneously or in sequence, together or separately?

Your analysis might suggest a change of strategy—that you should negotiate with a different party first, delay the deal or speed it up, bring others into the room, expand or contract the scope of the deal, and so on.

4. Control the Frame

The outcome of a negotiation depends a great deal on each side's leverage—the better your outside options are and the more ways you have to reward or coerce the other side, the more likely you are to achieve your objectives. But the psychology of the deal can be just as important.

In my experience, the frame, or psychological lens, through which the parties view the negotiation has a significant effect on where they end up. Are the parties treating the interaction as a problem-solving exercise or as a battle to be won? Are they looking at it as a meeting of equals, or do they perceive a difference in status? Are they focused on the long term or the short term? Are concessions expected, or are they seen as signs of weakness?

Effective negotiators will seek to control or adjust the frame early in the process—ideally, before the substance of the deal is even discussed. Here are three elements of framing that negotiators would be wise to consider.

Value versus price

I've worked with many technology companies whose innovative products provide tremendous value for customers but are priced significantly higher than what their competitors are charging—or what customers are paying for their legacy systems. While the high price is justified by the value proposition, salespeople often face immediate resistance when a potential customer learns that the cost will be five or 10 times the amount he is currently paying. Too often, the salesperson will hear something like: "You are charging five times what others charge. No one pays that much for this kind of thing!"

One of the most common mistakes salespeople make in those situations—without even realizing it—is to apologize for having a high price. They do this when they say "I understand it's pricey, but . . ." or when they hastily signal a willingness to adjust the price. My advice: Always justify your offer, but never apologize for it. When you apologize, you signal that even you don't think the price is appropriate, and you give the other side license to haggle. The entire frame of the negotiation becomes about price, when what you really want to discuss is value.

A better response would be, "What you seem to be asking is, How is it that despite a higher price, we still have a long and growing list of customers? We both know that no one will pay more for something than it's worth, so let's discuss the value we bring so that you can decide what's best for you."

In negotiations of all kinds, the sooner you can shift the discussion away from the cost to your counterpart and focus on the value you bring to the table, the more likely it is that you will be able to monetize that value.

Your alternatives versus theirs

Research and experience suggest that people who walk into a negotiation consumed by the question "what will happen to me if there is no deal?" get worse outcomes than those who focus on what would happen to the other side if there's no deal. When you are overly concerned with your own alternatives, and especially when your outside options are weak, you think in terms of "what will it take (at a minimum) to get them to say yes?" When you make the negotiation about what happens to them if there is no deal, you shift the frame to the unique value you offer, and it becomes easier to justify why you deserve a good deal.

Equality versus dominance

Not so long ago I was consulting on a strategic deal in which our side was a small, early-stage company and the other was a large multinational. One of the most important things we did throughout the process—and especially at the outset—was make sure the difference in company size did not frame the negotiation. I told our team, "These folks negotiate with two kinds of companies—those they consider their equals and those they think should feel lucky just to be at the table with them. And they treat the two kinds very differently, regardless of what they bring to the table." Over the years, I've seen many large organizations impose demands on their perceived inferiors that they'd never require from those they considered equals. In this negotiation, I wanted to make sure our counterpart treated us like equals.

To keep the dominance frame from taking hold, we started shaping expectations and perceptions at the very beginning, before we even considered the economics of the deal. For example, any time our counterpart made a procedural demand—however small—that we felt they would not have made of an equal, we respectfully pushed back on it. Any time they included a provision in the term sheet that seemed one-sided, even if it would not have been a costly concession, we redrafted it to be symmetrical. And throughout the negotiation, we made sure they understood that although our firm was much smaller, we were equals in this negotiation because of the tremendous value we offered. While I am not an advocate of nitpicking on minor issues, in this case we did so intentionally to help set the right frame.

Negotiators can shape the frame in countless other ways and on many other dimensions. At the very least, you want to ensure that the psychological lens that takes hold respects the value you bring to the table.

In *The Art of War*, Sun Tzu posits that every war is won or lost before it even begins. There is truth to this sentiment in most strategic interactions. While it would be unwise for negotiators to minimize the importance of carefully managing the substance of a deal, they should make every effort to avoid the mistakes that can occur before anyone has even formulated an offer. By paying attention to the four factors discussed here, you increase your chances of creating more-productive interactions and achieving more-profitable outcomes.

Originally published in December 2015. Reprint R1512D

Emotion and the Art of Negotiation

by Alison Wood Brooks

IT IS, WITHOUT QUESTION, my favorite day of the semester—the day when I teach my MBA students a negotiation exercise called "Honoring the Contract."

I assign students to partners, and each reads a different account of a (fictitious) troubled relationship between a supplier (a manufacturer of computer components) and a client (a search engine start-up). They learn that the two parties signed a detailed contract eight months earlier, but now they're at odds over several of the terms (sales volume, pricing, product reliability, and energy efficiency specs). Each student assumes the role of either client or supplier and receives confidential information about company finances and politics. Then each pair is tasked with renegotiating—a process that could lead to an amended deal, termination of the contract, or expensive litigation.

What makes this simulation interesting, however, lies not in the details of the case but in the top-secret instructions given to one side of each pairing before the exercise begins: "Please start the negotiation with a display of anger. You must display anger for a minimum of 10 minutes at the beginning." The instructions go on to give specific tips for showing anger: Interrupt the other party. Call her "unfair" or "unreasonable." Blame her personally for the disagreement. Raise your voice.

Before the negotiations begin, I spread the pairs all over the building so that the students can't see how others are behaving. Then, as the pairs negotiate, I walk around and observe. Although some students struggle, many are spectacularly good at feigning anger. They wag a finger in their partner's face. They pace around. I've never seen the exercise result in a physical confrontation—but it has come close. Some of the negotiators who did not get the secret instructions react by trying to defuse the other person's anger. But some react angrily themselves—and it's amazing how quickly the emotional responses escalate. When I bring everyone back into the classroom after 30 minutes, there are always students still yelling at each other or shaking their heads in disbelief.

During the debriefing, we survey the pairs to see how angry they felt and how they fared in resolving the problem. Often, the more anger the parties showed, the more likely it was that the negotiation ended poorly—for example, in litigation or an impasse (no deal). Once I've clued the entire class in on the setup, discussion invariably makes its way to this key insight: Bringing anger to a negotiation is like throwing a bomb into the process, and it's apt to have a profound effect on the outcome.

Until 20 years ago, few researchers paid much attention to the role of emotions in negotiating—how feelings can influence the way people overcome conflict, reach agreement, and create value when dealing with another party. Instead, negotiation scholars focused primarily on strategy and tactics—particularly the ways in which parties can identify and consider alternatives, use leverage, and execute the choreography of offers and counteroffers. Scientific understanding of negotiation also tended to home in on the transactional nature of working out a deal: how to get the most money or profit from the process. Even when experts started looking at psychological influences on negotiations, they focused on diffuse and nonspecific moods—such as whether negotiators felt generally positive or negative, and how that affected their behavior.

Over the past decade, however, researchers have begun examining how specific emotions—anger, sadness, disappointment, anxiety, envy, excitement, and regret—can affect the behavior of negotiators. They've studied the differences between what happens when people simply feel these emotions and what happens when

Idea in Brief

The Problem

Negotiators typically focus on strategy, tactics, offers, and counteroffers and don't pay enough attention to how emotions affect what happens at the bargaining table.

New Findings

Research shows that we can regulate the anxiety, anger, excitement, disappointment, or regret we may feel and express in the course of a negotiation—and doing so can help us make better deals.

Recommendations

Be aware of the emotions that negotiators commonly experience and how displays of emotion may be perceived. Then take specific steps to respond. For example, feeling or looking anxious weakens your bargaining power, so prepare and rehearse to stay calm, or ask a third party to negotiate for you.

they also express them to the other party through words or actions. In negotiations that are less transactional and involve parties in long-term relationships, understanding the role of emotions is even more important than it is in transactional deal making.

This new branch of research is proving extremely useful. We all have the ability to regulate how we experience emotions, and specific strategies can help us improve tremendously in that regard. We also have some control over the extent to which we express our feelings—and again, there are specific ways to cloak (or emphasize) an expression of emotion when doing so may be advantageous. For instance, research shows that feeling or looking anxious results in suboptimal negotiation outcomes. So individuals who are prone to anxiety when brokering a deal can take certain steps both to limit their nervousness and to make it less obvious to their negotiation opponent. The same is true for other emotions.

In the pages that follow, I discuss—and share coping strategies for—many of the emotions people typically feel over the course of a negotiation. Anxiety is most likely to crop up before the process begins or during its early stages. We're prone to experience anger or excitement in the heat of the discussions. And we're most likely to feel disappointment, sadness, or regret in the aftermath.

Avoiding Anxiety

Anxiety is a state of distress in reaction to threatening stimuli, particularly novel situations that have the potential for undesirable outcomes. In contrast to anger, which motivates people to escalate conflict (the "fight" part of the fight-or-flight response), anxiety trips the "flight" switch and makes people want to exit the scene.

Because patience and persistence are often desirable when negotiating, the urge to exit quickly is counterproductive. But the negative effects of feeling anxious while negotiating may go further. In my recent research, I wondered if anxious negotiators also develop low aspirations and expectations, which could lead them to make timid first offers—a behavior that directly predicts poor negotiating outcomes.

In work with Maurice Schweitzer in 2011, I explored how anxiety influences negotiations. First we surveyed 185 professionals about the emotions they expected to feel before negotiating with a stranger, negotiating to buy a car, and negotiating to increase their salary. When dealing with a stranger or asking for a higher salary, anxiety was the dominant emotional expectation; when negotiating for the car, anxiety was second only to excitement.

To understand how anxiety can affect negotiators, we then asked a separate group of 136 participants to negotiate a cell phone contract that required agreeing on a purchase price, a warranty period, and the length of the contract. We induced anxiety in half the participants by having them listen to continuous three-minute clips of the menacing theme music from the film *Psycho,* while the other half listened to pleasant music by Handel. (Researchers call this "incidental" emotional manipulation, and it's quite powerful. Listening to the *Psycho* music is genuinely uncomfortable: People's palms get sweaty, and some listeners become jumpy.)

In this experiment and three others, we found that anxiety had a significant effect on how people negotiated. People experiencing anxiety made weaker first offers, responded more quickly to each move the counterpart made, and were more likely to exit negotiations early (even though their instructions clearly warned that exiting early would reduce the value they received from the negotiation). Anxious negotiators made deals that were 12% less financially attractive than those made by negotiators in the neutral group. We did discover one caveat, however: People who gave themselves high ratings in a survey on negotiating aptitude were less affected by anxiety than others.

Those experiments examined what happens when people feel anxious. But what happens when they express that anxiety, making it clear to their counterparts that they're nervous (and perhaps vulnerable)? In 2012, with Francesca Gino and Maurice Schweitzer, I conducted eight experiments to explore how anxious people behaved in situations in which they could seek advice from others. We found that relative to people who did not feel anxious, they were less confident, more likely to consult others when making decisions, and less able to discriminate between good and bad advice. In the most relevant of these experiments, we found that anxious participants did not discount advice from someone with a stated conflict of interest, whereas subjects feeling neutral emotions looked upon that advice skeptically. Although this research didn't directly address how the subjects would negotiate, it suggests that people who express anxiety are more likely to be taken advantage of in a negotiation, especially if the other party senses their distress.

Excellent negotiators often make their counterparts feel anxious on purpose. For example, on the TV show *Shark Tank,* six wealthy investors (sharks) negotiate with entrepreneurs hoping for funding. The entrepreneurs must pitch their ideas in front of a huge television audience and face questions from the investors that are often aggressive and unnerving. As this is going on, stress-inducing music fills the TV studio. This setup does more than create drama and entertainment for viewers; it also intentionally puts pressure on the entrepreneurs. The sharks are professional negotiators who want to knock the entrepreneurs off balance so that it will be easier to take ownership of their good ideas at the lowest price possible. (When multiple sharks want to invest, they often drop comments that are intended to make opposing investors anxious too.) If you watch the show closely, you'll probably notice a pattern: The entrepreneurs who seem least rattled by the environmental stressors tend to negotiate the most carefully and deliberately—and often strike the best deals.

Managing Your Counterpart's Emotions

NEGOTIATING IS AN INTERPERSONAL PROCESS. There will always be at least one other party (and often many more) involved. In the adjoining article I discuss how to manage your own emotions during a negotiation. But what about the other people at the table? Can you manage their emotions as well? I suggest two strategies for doing so.

1. Be observant.

Perceiving how other people are feeling is a critical component of emotional intelligence, and it's particularly key in negotiations (as Adam Galinsky and his colleagues have found). So tune in to your counterpart's body language, tone of voice, and choice of words. When her verbal and nonverbal cues don't match up, ask questions. For example, "You are telling me you like this outcome, but you seem uneasy. Is something making you uncomfortable?" Or "You say you're angry, but you seem somewhat pleased. Are you truly upset about something? Or are you trying to intimidate me?"

Asking pointed questions based on your perceptions of the other party's emotional expressions will make it easier for you to understand her perspective (a task people are shockingly bad at, according to research by Nicholas

---

The takeaway from both research and practice is clear: Try your utmost to avoid feeling anxious while negotiating. How can you manage that? Train, practice, rehearse, and keep sharpening your negotiating skills. Anxiety is often a response to novel stimuli, so the more familiar the stimuli, the more comfortable and the less anxious you will feel. (That's why clinicians who treat anxiety disorders often rely on exposure therapy: People who are nervous about flying on airplanes, for instance, are progressively exposed to the experience, first getting used to the sights and sounds, then sitting in airliner seats, and ultimately taking flights.) Indeed, although many people enroll in negotiation classes to learn strategies and increase skills, one of the primary benefits is the comfort that comes from repeatedly practicing deal making in simulations and exercises. Negotiation eventually feels more routine, so it's not such an anxiety-inducing experience.

Another useful strategy for reducing anxiety is to bring in an outside expert to handle the bargaining. Third-party negotiators will be less anxious because their skills are better honed, the process is

Epley). It will also make it difficult for a counterpart to lie to you; evidence suggests that people prefer to tell lies of omission about facts rather than lies of commission about feelings.

2. Don't be afraid to exert direct influence on your counterpart's emotions.

This may sound manipulative or even unscrupulous, but you can use this influence for good. For example, if your counterpart seems anxious or angry, injecting humor or empathetic reassurance can dramatically change the tone of the interaction. By the same token, if your counterpart seems overconfident or pushy, expressing well-placed anger can inspire a healthy dose of fear.

In recent research with Elizabeth Baily Wolf, I have found that it's possible to go even further in managing others' emotions: You display an emotion, your counterpart sees it, and then you shape his interpretation of it. For example, imagine that you start crying at work. (Crying is a difficult-to-control and often embarrassing behavior.) Saying "I'm in tears because I'm passionate" rather than "I'm sorry I'm so emotional" can completely change the way others react and the way they view your self-control and competence.

routine for them, and they have a lower personal stake in the outcome. Outsourcing your negotiation may sound like a cop-out, but it's a frequent practice in many industries. Home buyers and sellers use real estate brokers partly for their negotiating experience; athletes, authors, actors, and even some business executives rely on agents to hammer out contracts. Although there are costs to this approach, they are often more than offset by the more favorable terms that can be achieved. And although anxious negotiators may have the most to gain from involving a third party (because anxiety can be a particularly difficult emotion to regulate in an uncomfortable setting), this strategy can also be useful when other negative emotions surface.

Managing Anger

Like anxiety, anger is a negative emotion, but instead of being self-focused, it's usually directed toward someone else. In most circumstances, we try to keep our tempers in check. When it comes to negotiating, however, many people believe that anger can be a productive emotion—one that will help them win a larger share of the pie.

This view stems from a tendency to view negotiations in competitive terms rather than collaborative ones. Researchers call this the fixed-pie bias: People, particularly those with limited experience making deals, assume that a negotiation is a zero-sum game in which their own interests conflict directly with a counterpart's. (More-experienced negotiators, in contrast, look for ways to expand the pie through collaboration, rather than nakedly trying to snatch a bigger slice.) Anger, the thinking goes, makes one seem stronger, more powerful, and better able to succeed in this grab for value.

In fact, there's a body of research—much of it by Keith Allred, a former faculty member at Harvard's Kennedy School of Government—that documents the consequences of feeling angry while negotiating. This research shows that anger often harms the process by escalating conflict, biasing perceptions, and making impasses more likely. It also reduces joint gains, decreases cooperation, intensifies competitive behavior, and increases the rate at which offers are rejected. Angry negotiators are less accurate than neutral negotiators both in recalling their own interests and in judging other parties' interests. And angry negotiators may seek to harm or retaliate against their counterparts, even though a more cooperative approach might increase the value that both sides can claim from the negotiation.

Despite these findings, many people continue to see advantages to feeling or appearing angry. Some even attempt to turn up the volume on their anger, because they think it will make them more effective in a negotiation. In my own research, I have found that given a choice between feeling angry and feeling happy while negotiating, more than half the participants want to be in an angry state and view it as significantly advantageous.

There *are* cases when feeling angry can lead to better outcomes. Research by Gerben van Kleef at the University of Amsterdam demonstrates that in a onetime, transactional negotiation with few opportunities to collaborate to create value, an angry negotiator can wind up with a better deal. There may even be situations in which a negotiator decides to feign anger, because the counterpart, in an attempt to defuse that anger, is likely to give ground on terms. This might work well if you are haggling with a stranger to buy a car, for example.

But negotiators who play this card must be aware of the costs. Showing anger in a negotiation damages the long-term relationship between the parties. It reduces liking and trust. Research by Rachel Campagna at the University of New Hampshire shows that false representations of anger may generate small tactical benefits but also lead to considerable and persistent blowback. That is, faking anger can create authentic feelings of anger, which in turn diminish trust for both parties. Along the same lines, research by Jeremy Yip and Martin Schweinsberg demonstrates that people who encounter an angry negotiator are more likely to walk away, preferring to let the process end in a stalemate.

In many contexts, then, feeling or expressing anger as a negotiating tactic can backfire. So in most cases, tamping down any anger you feel—and limiting the anger you express—is a smarter strategy. This may be hard to do, but there are tactics that can help.

Building rapport before, during, and after a negotiation can reduce the odds that the other party will become angry. If you seek to frame the negotiation cooperatively—to make it clear that you're seeking a win-win solution instead of trying to get the lion's share of a fixed pie—you may limit the other party's perception that an angry grab for value will work well. If the other party does become angry, apologize. Seek to soothe. Even if you feel that his anger is unwarranted, recognize that you're almost certainly better positioned tactically if you can reduce the hostility.

Perhaps the most effective way to deal with anger in negotiations is to recognize that many negotiations don't unfold all at once but take place over multiple meetings. So if tensions are flaring, ask for a break, cool off, and regroup. This isn't easy when you're angry, because your fight-or-flight response urges you to escalate, not pull back. Resist that urge and give the anger time to dissipate. In heated negotiations, hitting the pause button can be the smartest play.

Finally, you might consider reframing anger as sadness. Though reframing one negative emotion as another sounds illogical, shared feelings of sadness can lead to cooperative concession making, whereas oppositional anger often leads to an impasse.

Handling Disappointment and Regret

It can be tempting to see negotiations in binary terms—you either win or lose. Of course, that is generally too simplistic: Most complex negotiations will end with each side having achieved some of its goals and not others—a mix of wins and losses. Still, as a negotiation winds down, it's natural to look at the nascent agreement and feel, on balance, more positive or negative about it.

Disappointment can be a powerful force when it's expressed to the other party near the end of the negotiation. There's a relationship between anger and disappointment—both typically arise when an individual feels wronged—and it's useful to understand how one can be used more constructively than the other. (Think back to how you reacted as a child if your parents said "I'm very disappointed in you" instead of "I'm very angry with you.") Although expressing anger may create defensiveness or increase the odds of a standoff, expressing disappointment can serve a more tactical purpose by encouraging the other party to look critically at her own actions and consider whether she wants to change her position to reduce the negative feelings she's caused you.

Research shows that one cause of disappointment in a negotiation is the speed of the process. When a negotiation unfolds or concludes too quickly, participants tend to feel dissatisfied. They wonder if they could or should have done more or pushed harder. Negotiation teachers see this in class exercises: Often the first students to finish up are the most disappointed by the outcome. The obvious way to lessen the likelihood of disappointment is to proceed slowly and deliberately.

Regret is slightly different from disappointment. While the latter tends to involve sadness about an outcome, someone feeling regret is looking a little more upstream, at the course of actions that led to

Preparing Your Emotional Strategy

PREPARATION IS KEY TO SUCCESS in negotiations. It's vital to give advance thought to the objective factors involved (Who are the parties? What are the issues? What is my best outside option if we don't reach a deal?), but it is perhaps even more important to prepare your emotional strategy. Use the following questions and tips to plan ahead for each stage of the negotiation.

	Ask yourself:	Remember:
The buildup	• How do I feel? • Should I express my emotions? • How might the people across the table feel? • Are they likely to hide or express their emotions? • Should I recruit a third party to negotiate on my behalf?	• It's normal to feel anxious and excited. • Try to avoid expressing anxiety. • Expressing forward-looking excitement may help build rapport. • In emotionally charged situations (such as a divorce), consider having a third party (such as a lawyer) negotiate on your behalf.
The main event	• What things could happen that would make me feel angry? • What things might I do that would trigger my counterparts to feel angry? • What might they do or ask that would make me feel anxious?	• Be careful about expressing anger; it may extract concessions but harm the long-term relationship. • Avoid angering your counterparts; they are likely to walk away. • Preparing answers to tough questions is critical for staying calm in the moment.
The finale	• What are the possible outcomes of the negotiation? What do I hope to achieve? What do I expect to achieve? • How would those outcomes make me feel? • Should I express those feelings? To whom? • How are my counterparts likely to feel about the possible outcomes?	• To reduce disappointment, outline clear aspirations and expectations and adjust them throughout the negotiation. • When you feel pleased about an outcome, it may be wise to keep it to yourself. • The best negotiators create value for everyone, claiming the lion's share for themselves but making their counterparts feel that they, too, won.

this unhappy outcome, and thinking about the missteps or mistakes that created the disappointment.

Research shows that people are most likely to regret actions they didn't take—the missed opportunities and errors of omission, rather than errors of commission. That can be a powerful insight for negotiators, whose primary actions should be asking questions, listening, proposing solutions, and brainstorming new alternatives if the parties can't agree. Ironically, people often don't ask questions while negotiating: They may forget to raise important matters or feel reluctant to probe too deeply, deeming it invasive or rude. Those fears are often misplaced. In fact, people who ask a lot of questions tend to be better liked, and they learn more things. In negotiations, information is king and learning should be a central goal. One way to reduce the potential for regret is to ask questions without hesitation. Aim to come away from the negotiation with the sense that every avenue was explored.

Skilled negotiators use another technique to minimize the odds of regret: the "post-settlement settlement." This strategy recognizes that tension often dissipates when there's a deal on the table that makes everyone happy, and sometimes the best negotiating happens after that tension is released. So instead of shaking hands and ending the deal making, one party might say, "We're good. We have terms we can all live with. But now that we know we've reached an agreement, let's spend a few more minutes chatting to see if we can find anything that sweetens it for both sides." Done ineptly, this might seem as if one party is trying to renege or renegotiate. However, when handled deftly, a post-settlement settlement can open a pathway for both sides to become even more satisfied with the outcome and stave off regrets.

Tempering Happiness and Excitement

There isn't much research on how happiness and excitement affect negotiations, but intuition and experience suggest that expressing these emotions can have significant consequences. The National Football League prohibits and penalizes "excessive celebrations" after a touchdown or big play because such conduct can generate ill will. For the same reason, the "winner" in a deal should not gloat as the negotiations wrap up. Nonetheless, this happens all the time: In workshops I routinely see students unabashedly boast and brag (sometimes to the entire class) about how they really stuck it to their opponents in a negotiation exercise. Not only do these students risk looking like jerks, but in a real-world setting they might suffer more-dire consequences, such as the other party's invoking a right of rescission, seeking to renegotiate, or taking punitive action the next time the parties need to strike a deal.

Although it's unpleasant to feel disappointed after a negotiation, it can be even worse to make your counterparts feel that way. And in certain situations, showing happiness or excitement triggers disappointment in others. The best negotiators achieve great deals for themselves but leave their opponents believing that they, too, did fabulously, even if the truth is different. In deals that involve a significant degree of future collaboration—say, when two companies agree to merge, or when an actor signs a contract with a producer to star in an upcoming movie—it can be appropriate to show excitement, but it's important to focus on the opportunities ahead rather than the favorable terms one party just gained.

Another danger of excitement is that it may increase your commitment to strategies or courses of action that you'd be better off abandoning. In my negotiation class, we do an exercise in which students must decide whether or not to send a race car driver into an important race with a faulty engine. Despite the risks, most students opt to go ahead with the race because they are excited and want to maximize their prize winnings. The exercise has parallels to a real-life example: the launch of the *Challenger* space shuttle. Though the engineers who designed the *Challenger*'s faulty O-ring had qualms about it, NASA managers were overly excited and determined to proceed with the launch. Their decision ultimately led to the craft's explosion and the loss of its seven crew members.

There are two lessons for negotiators. First, be considerate: Do not let your excitement make your counterparts feel that they lost. Second, be skeptical: Do not let your excitement lead to overconfidence or an escalation of commitment with insufficient data.

Negotiating requires some of the same skills that playing poker does—a strategic focus, the imagination to see alternatives, and a knack for assessing odds, reading people, understanding others' positions, and bluffing when necessary. However, whereas the parties in a negotiation must strive for agreement, poker players make decisions unilaterally. Poker also lacks win-win outcomes or pie-sharing strategies: Any given hand is generally a zero-sum game, with one player's gains coming directly from the other players' pots.

Nonetheless, negotiators can learn a crucial lesson from the card table: the value of controlling the emotions we feel and especially those we reveal. In other words, good negotiators need to develop a poker face—not one that remains expressionless, always hiding true feelings, but one that displays the right emotions at the right times.

And although all human beings experience emotions, the frequency and intensity with which we do so differs from person to person. To be a better deal maker, conduct a thorough assessment of which emotions you are particularly prone to feel before, during, and after negotiations, and use techniques to minimize (or maximize) the experience and suppress (or emphasize) the expression of emotions as needed.

In one of my favorite scenes from the TV show *30 Rock,* the hard-driving CEO Jack Donaghy (Alec Baldwin), who fancies himself an expert negotiator, explains to a colleague why he struck a poor deal: "I lost because of emotion, which I always thought was a weakness, but now I have learned can also be a weapon." Borrowing Jack's insightful metaphor, I urge you to wield your emotions thoughtfully. Think carefully about when to draw these weapons, when to shoot, and when to keep them safely tucked away in a hidden holster. Try to avoid feeling anxious, be careful about expressing anger, ask questions to circumvent disappointment and regret, and remember that happiness and excitement can have adverse consequences.

Just as you prepare your tactical and strategic moves before a negotiation, you should invest effort in preparing your emotional approach. It will be time well spent.

Originally published in December 2015. Reprint R1512C

Breakthrough Bargaining

by Deborah M. Kolb and Judith Williams

NEGOTIATION WAS ONCE CONSIDERED AN ART practiced by the naturally gifted. To some extent it still is, but increasingly we in the business world have come to regard negotiation as a science—built on creative approaches to deal making that allow everyone to walk away winners of sorts. Executives have become experts at "getting to yes," as the now-familiar terminology goes.

Nevertheless, some negotiations stall or, worse, never get off the ground. Why? Our recent research suggests that the answers lie in a dynamic we have come to call the "shadow negotiation"—the complex and subtle game people play before they get to the table and continue to play after they arrive. The shadow negotiation doesn't determine the "what" of the discussion, but the "how." Which interests will hold sway? Will the conversation's tone be adversarial or cooperative? Whose opinions will be heard? In short, how will bargainers deal with each other?

The shadow negotiation is most obvious when the participants hold unequal power—say, subordinates asking bosses for more resources or new employees engaging with veterans about well-established company policies. Similarly, managers who, because of their race, age, or gender, are in the minority in their companies may be at a disadvantage in the shadow negotiation. Excluded from important networks, they may not have the personal clout, experience, or organizational standing to influence other parties. Even when the bargainers are peers, a negotiation can be blocked or stalled—undermined by hidden assumptions, unrealistic expectations, or personal histories. An unexamined shadow negotiation can lead to silence, not satisfaction.

It doesn't have to be that way. Our research identified strategic levers—we call them power moves, process moves, and appreciative moves—that executives can use to guide the shadow negotiation. In situations in which the other person sees no compelling need to negotiate, *power moves* can help bring him or her to the table. When the dynamics of decision making threaten to overpower a negotiator's voice, *process moves* can reshape the negotiation's structure. And when talks stall because the other party feels pushed or misunderstandings cloud the real issues, *appreciative moves* can alter the tone or atmosphere so that a more collaborative exchange is possible. These strategic moves don't guarantee that bargainers will walk away winners, but they help to get stalled negotiations out of the dark of unspoken power plays and into the light of true dialogue.

Power Moves

In the informal negotiations common in the workplace, one of the parties can be operating from a one-down position. The other bargainer, seeing no apparent advantage in negotiating, stalls. Phone calls go unanswered. The meeting keeps being postponed or, if it does take place, a two-way conversation never gets going. Ideas are ignored or overruled, demands dismissed. Such resistance is a natural part of the informal negotiation process. A concern will generally be accorded a fair hearing only when someone believes two things: the other party has something desirable, and one's own objectives will not be met without giving something in return. Willingness to negotiate is, therefore, a confession of mutual need. As a result, a primary objective in the shadow negotiation is fostering the perception of mutual need.

Power moves can bring reluctant bargainers to the realization that they must negotiate: they will be better off if they do and worse

Idea in Brief

Unspoken, subtle parts of a bargaining process—also known as the shadow negotiation—can set the tone for a successful negotiation. Deborah Kolb and Judith Williams, whose book *The Shadow Negotiation* was the starting point for this article, say there are three strategies businesspeople can use to guide these hidden interactions.

Power moves are used when two negotiating parties hold unequal power. These strategies, such as casting the status quo in an unfavorable light, can help parties realize that they must negotiate: they will be better off if they do and worse off if they don't.

Process moves affect how negotiation issues are received by both sides in the process, even though they do not address substantive issues. Working outside of the actual bargaining process, one party can suggest ideas or marshal support that can shape the agenda and influence how others view the negotiation.

Appreciative moves alter the tone or atmosphere so that a more collaborative exchange is possible. They shift the dynamic of the shadow negotiation away from the adversarial—helping to save face—and thus build trust and encourage dialogue.

These strategic moves don't guarantee that all bargainers will walk away winners, but they help to get stalled negotiations moving—out of the dark of unspoken power plays and into the light of true dialogue.

off if they don't. Bargainers can use three kinds of power moves. Incentives emphasize the proposed value to the other person and the advantage to be gained from negotiating. Pressure levers underscore the consequences to the other side if stalling continues. And the third power move, enlisting allies, turns up the volume on the incentives or on the pressure. Here's how these strategies work.

Offer incentives

In any negotiation, the other party controls something the bargainer needs: money, time, cooperation, communication, and so on. But the bargainer's needs alone aren't enough to bring anyone else to the table. The other side must recognize that benefits will accrue from the negotiation. These benefits must not only be visible—that

About the Research

WE BECAME AWARE of the shadow negotiation as we interviewed, over a five-year period, more than 300 executive women to probe their work experiences in formal and informal negotiations. We spoke with lawyers and bankers, accountants and entrepreneurs, consultants and marketers, project managers and account executives across a range of industries and organizational types. In each interview, we asked about the executive's best and worst negotiation experience. After describing these scenarios, the women wanted to talk with us not only about what worked and why but also about how they might have better handled challenging situations.

During this interviewing and the subsequent writing of *The Shadow Negotiation*, we came to believe that these dialogues and the study's findings have implications for both men and women. The shadow negotiation is where issues of parity, or the equivalence of power, get settled. And parity—its presence or absence—determines to a great extent whether a negotiation takes place at all and on what terms.

is, right there on the table—but they must also resonate with the other side's needs. High-tech executive Fiona Sweeney quickly recognized this dynamic when she tried to initiate informal talks about a mission-critical organizational change.

Shortly after being promoted to head operations at an international systems company, Sweeney realized that the organization's decision-making processes required fundamental revamping. The company operated through a collection of fiefdoms, with little coordination even on major accounts. Sales managers, whose bonuses were tied to gross sales, pursued any opportunity with minimal regard for the company's ability to deliver. Production scrambled to meet unrealistic schedules; budgets and quality suffered. Sweeney had neither the authority nor the inclination to order sales and production to cooperate. And as a newcomer to corporate headquarters, her visibility and credibility were low.

Sweeney needed a sweetener to bring sales and production together. First, she made adjustments to the billing process, reducing errors from 7.1% to 2.4% over a three-month period, thereby cutting back on customer complaints. Almost immediately, her stock shot up with both of the divisions. Second, realizing that sales would be more reluctant than production to negotiate any changes in the organization's decision-making processes, she worked with billing to speed up processing the expense-account checks so that salespeople were reimbursed more quickly, a move that immediately got the attention of everyone in sales. By demonstrating her value to sales and production, Sweeney encouraged the two division managers to work with her on improving their joint decision-making process. (For the complete story of Fiona Sweeney's campaign to revamp operations, see the sidebar "The Shadow Campaign.")

Creating value and making it visible are key power moves in the shadow negotiation. A bargainer can't leave it up to the other party to puzzle through the possibilities. The benefits must be made explicit if they are to have any impact on the shadow negotiation. When value disappears, so do influence and bargaining power.

Put a price on the status quo

Abba Eban, Israel's former foreign minister, once observed that diplomats have "a passionate love affair with the status quo" that blocks any forward movement. The same love affair carries over into ordinary negotiations in the workplace. When people believe that a negotiation has the potential to produce bad results for them, they are naturally reluctant to engage on the issues. Until the costs of *not* negotiating are made explicit, ducking the problem will be the easier or safer course.

To unlock the situation, the status quo must be perceived as less attractive. By exerting pressure, the bargainer can raise the cost of business-as-usual until the other side begins to see that things will get worse unless both sides get down to talking.

That is exactly what Karen Hartig, one of the women in our study, did when her boss dragged his heels about giving her a raise. Not only had she been promoted without additional pay, but she was now doing two jobs because the first position had never been filled. Although her boss continued to assure her of his support, nothing changed. Finally, Hartig was so exasperated that she returned a headhunter's call. The resulting job offer provided her with enough leverage to unfreeze the talks with her boss. No longer could he

The Shadow Campaign

A SINGLE STRATEGIC MOVE seldom carries the day. In combination, however, such moves can jump-start workplace negotiations and keep them moving toward resolution.

Consider the case of Fiona Sweeney, the new operations chief introduced earlier in this article. She had neither the authority nor the personal inclination to order the sales and production divisions of her company to cooperate. Instead, she fashioned a series of strategic moves designed to influence the negotiations.

Power Moves

Having established her credibility with sales by increasing the turnaround time on expense-account reimbursements, Sweeney knew she needed to up the ante for maintaining the status quo, which created hardships for production and was frustrating customers. It was particularly important to bring pressure to bear on the sales division, since the informal reward systems, and many of the formal ones, currently worked to its benefit. To disturb the equilibrium, Sweeney began to talk in management meetings about a bonus system that would penalize the sales division whenever it promised more than production could deliver. Rather than immediately acting on this threat, however, she suggested creating a cross-divisional task force to explore the issues. Not surprisingly, sales was eager to be included. Moreover, the CEO let key people know that he backed Sweeney's proposal to base bonuses on profits, not revenues.

Process Moves

Sweeney then moved to exert control over the agenda and build support for the changes she and the CEO envisioned. She started an operations subgroup with the heads of quality control and production, mobilizing allies in the two areas

---

afford to maintain the status quo. By demonstrating that she had another alternative, she gave him the push—and the justification—he needed to argue forcefully on her behalf with his boss and with human resources.

Enlist support

Solo power moves won't always do the job. Another party may not see sufficient benefits to negotiating, or the potential costs may not be high enough to compel a change of mind. When incentives and

most directly affected by the sales division's behavior. Soon they developed a common agenda and began working in concert to stem the influence of sales in senior staff meetings. On one occasion, for example, Sweeney proposed assigning a low priority to orders that had not been cleared by the operations subgroup. Quality control and production roundly supported the suggestion, which was soon implemented. Through these process moves, Sweeney built a coalition that shaped the subsequent negotiations. But she did something more.

Power and process moves often provoke resistance from the other side. Sweeney prevented resistance from becoming entrenched within the sales division through a series of appreciative moves.

Appreciative Moves

To deepen her understanding of the issues sales confronted, Sweeney volunteered her operations expertise to the division's planning team. By helping sales develop a new pricing-and-profit model, she not only increased understanding and trust on both sides of the table, but she also paved the way for dialogue on other issues—specifically the need for change in the company's decision-making processes.

Most important, Sweeney never forced any of the players into positions where they would lose face. By using a combination of strategic moves, she helped the sales division realize that change was coming and that it would be better off helping to shape the change than blocking it. In the end, improved communication and cooperation among divisions resulted in increases in both the company's top-line revenues and its profit margins. With better product quality and delivery times, sales actually made more money, and production no longer had the burden of delivering on unrealistic promises generated by sales. Customers—and the CEO—were all happy.

pressure levers fail to move the negotiation forward, a bargainer can enlist the help of allies.

Allies are important resources in shadow negotiations. They can be crucial in establishing credibility, and they lend tangible support to incentives already proposed. By providing guidance or running interference, they can favorably position a bargainer's proposals before talks even begin. At a minimum, their confidence primes the other party to listen and raises the costs of not negotiating seriously.

When a member of Dan Riley's squadron faced a prolonged family emergency, the air force captain needed to renegotiate his squadron's flight-rotation orders. The matter was particularly sensitive, however, because it required the consent of the wing commander, two levels up the chain of command. If Riley approached the commander directly, he risked making his immediate superior look bad since his responsibilities covered readiness planning. To bridge that difficulty, Riley presented a draft proposal to his immediate superior. Once aware of the problem, Riley and his superior anticipated some of the objections the commander might raise and then alerted the wing commander to the general difficulties posed by such situations. When Riley finally presented his proposal to the commander, it carried his immediate superior's blessing, and so his credibility was never questioned; only the merits of his solution were discussed.

Process Moves

Rather than attempt to influence the shadow negotiation directly through power moves, a bargainer can exercise another kind of strategic move, the process move. Designed to influence the negotiation process itself, such moves can be particularly effective when bargainers are caught in a dynamic of silencing—when decisions are being made without their input or when colleagues interrupt them during meetings, dismiss their comments, or appropriate their ideas.

While process moves do not address the substantive issues in a negotiation, they directly affect the hearing those issues receive. The agenda, the prenegotiation groundwork, and the sequence in which ideas and people are heard—all these structural elements influence others' receptivity to opinions and demands. Working behind the scenes, a bargainer can plant the seeds of ideas or marshal support before a position becomes fixed in anyone's mind. Consensus can even be engineered so that the bargainer's agenda frames the subsequent discussion.

Seed ideas early

Sometimes parties to a negotiation simply shut down and don't listen; for whatever reason, they screen out particular comments or people. Being ignored in a negotiation doesn't necessarily result from saying too little or saying it too hesitantly. When ideas catch people off guard, they can produce negative, defensive reactions, as can ideas presented too forcefully. Negotiators also screen out the familiar: if they've already heard the speech, or a close variant, they stop paying attention.

Joe Lopez faced this dilemma. Lopez, a fast-track engineer who tended to promote his ideas vigorously in planning meetings, began to notice that his peers were tuning him out—a serious problem since departmental resources were allocated in these sessions. To remedy the situation, Lopez scheduled one-on-one lunch meetings with his colleagues. On each occasion, he mentioned how a particular project would benefit the other manager's department and how they could work together to ensure its completion. As a result of this informal lobbying, Lopez found he no longer needed to oversell his case in the meetings. He could make his ideas heard with fewer words and at a lower decibel level.

Preliminary work like this allows a bargainer to build receptivity where a direct or aggressive approach might encounter resistance. Once the seeds of an idea have been planted, they will influence how others view a situation, regardless of how firmly attached they are to their own beliefs and ideas.

Reframe the process

Negotiators are not equally adept in all settings. Highly competitive approaches to problem solving favor participants who can bluff and play the game, talk the loudest, hold out the longest, and think fastest on their feet. Bargainers who are uncomfortable with this kind of gamesmanship can reframe the process, shifting the dynamic away from personal competition. That's what Marcia Philbin decided to do about the way in which space was allocated in her company. Extra room and equipment typically went to those who pushed the hardest, and Philbin never fared well in the negotiations. She also believed that significant organizational costs always accompanied the process since group leaders routinely presented the building administrator with inflated figures, making it impossible to assess the company's actual requirements.

Positioning herself as an advocate not only for her department but also for the company, Philbin proposed changing the process. Rather than allocating space in a series of discrete negotiations with the space administrator, she suggested, why not collaborate as a group in developing objective criteria for assessing need? Management agreed, and Philbin soon found herself chairing the committee created to produce the new guidelines. Heated arguments took place over the criteria, but Philbin was now positioned to direct the discussions away from vested and parochial interests toward a greater focus on organizational needs.

Within organizations or groups, negotiations can fall into patterns. If a bargainer's voice is consistently shut out of discussions, something about the way negotiations are structured is working against his or her active participation. A process move may provide a remedy because it will influence how the discussion unfolds and how issues emerge.

Build consensus

Regardless of how high a bargainer is on the organizational ladder, it is not always possible—or wise—to impose change on a group by fiat. By lobbying behind the scenes, a bargainer can start to build consensus before formal decision making begins. Unlike the first process move, which aims at gaining a hearing for ideas, building consensus creates momentum behind an agenda by bringing others on board. The growing support isolates the blockers, making continued opposition harder and harder. Moreover, once agreement has been secured privately, it becomes difficult (although never impossible) for a supporter to defect publicly.

As CEO of a rapidly growing biotechnology company, Mark Chapin gradually built consensus for his ideas on integrating a newly acquired research boutique into the existing company. Chapin had two goals: to retain the acquired firm's scientific talent and to rationalize the research funding process. The second goal was at odds with the first and threatened to alienate the new scientists. To mitigate this potential conflict, Chapin focused his attention on the shadow negotiation. First, he met one-on-one with key leaders of the board and the research staffs of both companies. These private talks provided him with a strategic map that showed where he would find support and where he was likely to meet challenges. Second, in another round of talks, Chapin paid particular attention to the order in which he approached people. Beginning with the most supportive person, he got the key players to commit, one by one, to his agenda before opposing factions could coalesce. These preliminary meetings positioned him as a collaborator—and, equally important, as a source of expanding research budgets. Having privately built commitment, Chapin found that he didn't need to use his position to dictate terms when the principal players finally sat down to negotiate the integration plan.

Appreciative Moves

Power moves exert influence on the other party so that talks get off the ground. Process moves seek to change the ground rules under which negotiations play out. But still, talks may stall. Two strong advocates may have backed themselves into respective corners. Or one side, put on the defensive, even inadvertently, may continue to resist or raise obstacles. Communication may deteriorate, turn acrimonious, or simply stop as participants focus solely on their own demands. Wariness stifles any candid exchange. And without candor, the two sides cannot address the issues together or uncover the real conflict.

Appreciative moves break these cycles. They explicitly build trust and encourage the other side to participate in a dialogue. Not only do appreciative moves shift the dynamics of the shadow negotiation away from the adversarial, but they also hold out a hidden promise. When bargainers demonstrate appreciation for another's concerns, situation, or "face," they open the negotiation to the different perspectives held by that person and to the opinions, ideas, and feelings shaping those perspectives. Appreciative moves foster open communication so that differences in needs and views can come to the surface without personal discord. Frequently the participants then discover that the problem they were worrying about is not the root conflict, but a symptom of it. And at times, before a negotiation can move toward a common solution, the participants must first experience mutuality, recognizing where their interests and needs intersect. A shared problem can then become the basis for creative problem solving.

Help others save face

Image is a concern for everyone. How negotiators look to themselves and to others who matter to them often counts as much as the particulars of an agreement. In fact, these are seldom separate. "Face" captures what people value in themselves and the qualities they want others to see in them. Negotiators go to great lengths to preserve face. They stick to their guns against poor odds simply to avoid losing face with those who are counting on them. If a bargainer treads on another's self-image—in front of a boss or colleague, or even privately—his or her demands are likely to be rejected.

Sensitivity to the other side's face does more than head off resistance: it lays the groundwork for trust. It conveys that the bargainer respects what the other is trying to accomplish and will not do anything to embarrass or undermine that person. This appreciation concedes nothing, yet as Sam Newton discovered, it can turn out to be the only way to break a stalemate.

Newton's new boss, transferred from finance, lacked experience on the operations side of the business. During departmental meetings to negotiate project schedules and funding, he always rejected Newton's ideas. Soon it was routine: Newton would make a suggestion, and before he got the last sentence out, his boss was issuing a categorical veto.

Frustrated, Newton pushed harder, only to meet increased resistance. Finally, he took a step back and looked at the situation from his boss's perspective. Rubber-stamping Newton's proposals could have appeared as a sign of weakness at a time when his boss was still establishing his credentials. From then on, Newton took a different tack. Rather than present a single idea, he offered an array of options and acknowledged that the final decision rested with his boss. Gradually, his boss felt less need to assert his authority and could respond positively in their dealings.

Bosses aren't the only ones who need to save face; colleagues and subordinates do, too. Team members avoid peers who bump a problem upstairs at the first sign of trouble, making everyone appear incapable of producing a solution. Subordinates muzzle their real opinions once they have been belittled or treated dismissively by superiors. In the workplace, attention to face is a show of respect for another person, whatever one's corporate role. That respect carries over to the shadow negotiation.

Keep the dialogue going

Sometimes, talks don't get off the ground because the timing is not right for a participant to make a decision; information may be insufficient, or he or she is simply not ready. People have good reasons—at least, reasons that make sense to them—for thinking it's not yet time to negotiate. Appreciating this disposition doesn't mean abandoning or postponing a negotiation. Instead, it requires that a bargainer keep the dialogue going without pushing for immediate agreement. This appreciative move allows an opportunity for additional information to come to the surface and affords the other side more time to rethink ideas and adjust initial predilections.

Francesca Rossi knew instinctively that unless she kept the communication lines open, discussions would derail about the best way for her software firm to grow. The company had recently decided to expand by acquiring promising applications rather than developing them in-house from scratch. As head of strategic development, Rossi targeted a small start-up that designed state-of-the-art software for office computers to control home appliances. The director of research, however, was less than enthusiastic about acquiring the firm. He questioned the product's commercial viability and argued that its market would never justify the acquisition cost.

Needing his cooperation, Rossi pulled back. Instead of actively promoting the acquisition, she began to work behind the scenes with the start-up's software designers and industry analysts. As Rossi gathered more data in support of the application's potential, she gradually drew the director of research back into the discussions. He dropped his opposition once the analysis convinced him that the acquisition, far from shrinking his department's authority, would actually enlarge it. Rossi's appreciative move had given him the additional information and time he needed to reevaluate his original position.

Not everyone makes decisions quickly. Sometimes people can't see beyond their initial ideas or biases. Given time to mull over the issues, they may eventually reverse course and be more amenable to negotiating. As long as the issue isn't forced or brought to a preemptive conclusion—as long as the participants keep talking—there's a chance that the resistance will fade. What seems unreasonable at one point in a negotiation can become more acceptable at another. Appreciative moves that keep the dialogue going allow the other side to progress at a comfortable speed.

Solicit new perspectives

One of the biggest barriers to effective negotiation and a major cause of stalemate is the tendency for bargainers to get trapped in their own perspectives. It's simply too easy for people to become overly enamored of their opinions. Operating in a closed world of their making, they tell themselves they are right and the other person is wrong. They consider the merits of their own positions but neglect the other party's valid objections. They push their agendas, merely reiterating the same argument, and may not pick up on cues that their words aren't being heard.

It's safe to assume that the other party is just as convinced that his or her own demands are justified. Moreover, bargainers can only speculate what another's agenda might be—hidden or otherwise. Appreciative moves to draw out another's perspectives help negotiators understand why the other party feels a certain way. But these moves serve more than an instrumental purpose, doing more than add information to a bargainer's arsenal. They signal to the other side that differing opinions and perspectives are important. By creating opportunities to discover something new and unexpected, appreciative moves can break a stalemate. As understanding deepens on both sides of the table, reaching a mutual resolution becomes increasingly possible.

Everyone agreed that a joint venture negotiated by HMO executive Donna Hitchcock between her organization and an insurance company dovetailed with corporate objectives on both sides. The HMO could expand its patient base and the insurance carrier its enrollment.

Although the deal looked good on paper, implementation stalled. Hitchcock couldn't understand where the resistance was coming from or why. In an attempt to unfreeze the situation, she arranged a meeting with her counterpart from the insurance company. After a brief update, Hitchcock asked about any unexpected effects the joint venture was exerting on the insurance carrier's organization and on her counterpart's work life. That appreciative move ultimately broke the logjam. From the carrier's perspective, she learned, the new arrangement stretched already overworked departments and had not yet produced additional revenues to hire more staff. Even more important, her counterpart was personally bearing the burden of the increased work.

Hitchcock was genuinely sympathetic to these concerns. The extra work was a legitimate obstacle to the joint venture's successful implementation. Once she understood the reason behind her counterpart's resistance, the two were able to strategize on ways to alleviate the overload until the additional revenues kicked in.

Through these appreciative moves—actively soliciting the other side's ideas and perspectives, acknowledging their importance, and demonstrating that they are taken seriously—negotiators can encourage the other person to work with them rather than against them.

There's more to negotiation than haggling over issues and working out solutions. The shadow negotiation, though often overlooked, is a critical component. Whether a bargainer uses power, process, or appreciative moves in the shadow negotiation depends on the demands of the situation. Power moves encourage another party to recognize the need to negotiate in the first place. They help bring a reluctant bargainer to the table. Process moves create a context in which a bargainer can shape the negotiation's agenda and dynamic so that he or she can be a more effective advocate. Appreciative moves engage the other party in a collaborative exchange by fostering trust and candor in the shadow negotiation. While power and process moves can ensure that a negotiation gets started on the right foot, appreciative moves can break a stalemate once a negotiation is under way. By broadening the discourse, appreciative moves can also lead to creative solutions. Used alone or in combination, strategic moves in the shadow negotiation can determine the outcome of the negotiation on the issues.

Originally printed in February 2001. Reprint R0102

Note

Most of the negotiating stories used in this article have been adapted from *The Shadow Negotiation: How Women Can Master the Hidden Agendas That Determine Bargaining Success* (Simon & Schuster, 2000) and the authors' interviews with businesspeople. To respect interviewees' candor and to protect their privacy, their identities and situations have been disguised, sometimes radically.

15 Rules for Negotiating a Job Offer

by Deepak Malhotra

JOB-OFFER NEGOTIATIONS are rarely easy. Consider three typical scenarios:

You're in a third-round interview for a job at a company you like, but a firm you admire even more just invited you in. Suddenly the first hiring manager cuts to the chase: "As you know, we're considering many candidates. We like you, and we hope the feeling is mutual. If we make you a competitive offer, will you accept it?"

You've received an offer for a job you'll enjoy, but the salary is lower than you think you deserve. You ask your potential boss whether she has any flexibility. "We typically don't hire people with your background, and we have a different culture here," she responds. "This job isn't just about the money. Are you saying you won't take it unless we increase the pay?"

You've been working happily at your company for three years, but a recruiter has been calling, insisting that you could earn much more elsewhere. You don't want to quit, but you expect to be compensated fairly, so you'd like to ask for a raise. Unfortunately, budgets are tight, and your boss doesn't react well when people try to leverage outside offers. What do you do?

Each of these situations is difficult in its own way—and emblematic of how complex job negotiations can be. At many companies, compensation increasingly comes in the form of stock, options, and bonuses linked to both personal and group performance. In MBA recruitment, more companies are using "exploding" offers or sliding-scale signing bonuses based on when a candidate accepts the job, complicating attempts to compare offers. With executive mobility on the rise, people vying for similar positions often have vastly different backgrounds, strengths, and salary histories, making it hard for employers to set benchmarks or create standard packages.

In some industries a weak labor market has also left candidates with fewer options and less leverage, and employers better positioned to dictate terms. Those who are unemployed, or whose current job seems shaky, have seen their bargaining power further reduced.

But job market complexity creates opportunities for people who can skillfully negotiate the terms and conditions of employment. After all, negotiation matters most when there is a broad range of possible outcomes.

As a professor who studies and teaches the subject, I frequently advise current and former students on navigating this terrain. For several years I have been offering a presentation on the topic to current students. (To see a video of this talk, go to www.NegotiateYourOffer .com.) Every situation is unique, but some strategies, tactics, and principles can help you address many of the issues people face in negotiating with employers. Here are 15 rules to guide you in these discussions.

The Rules

Don't underestimate the importance of likability

This sounds basic, but it's crucial: People are going to fight for you only if they like you. Anything you do in a negotiation that makes you less likable reduces the chances that the other side will work to get you a better offer. This is about more than

Idea in Brief

In some industries, a weak labor market has left candidates with fewer options and less leverage, and employers better positioned to dictate terms. Those who are unemployed, or whose current job seems shaky, have seen their bargaining power further reduced. But the complexity of the job market creates opportunities for people to negotiate the terms and conditions of employment. Negotiation matters most when there is a broad range of potential outcomes. There are 15 rules for negotiating a job offer. One is "don't underestimate the importance of likability," which means managing inevitable tensions in negotiation, being persistent without being a nuisance, and

understanding how other people perceive your approach. Another rule is "make it clear they can get you." Indicate that you're serious about working for a potential employer, and don't discourage them from trying to win you by suggesting you have too many better options. You should also "be prepared for tough questions," like "Are we your top choice?" Don't lie or try too hard to please, lest you lose your leverage. And "consider the whole deal," including the job's perks, location, opportunities for growth, and flexibility in work hours—not just the salary. These and other guidelines can help you attain the terms and conditions of employment you want.

being polite; it's about managing some inevitable tensions in negotiation, such as asking for what you deserve without seeming greedy, pointing out deficiencies in the offer without seeming petty, and being persistent without being a nuisance. Negotiators can typically avoid these pitfalls by evaluating (for example, in practice interviews with friends) how others are likely to perceive their approach.

Help them understand why you deserve what you're requesting

It's not enough for them to like you. They also have to believe you're worth the offer you want. Never let your proposal speak for itself—always tell the story that goes with it. Don't just state your desire (a 15% higher salary, say, or permission to work from home one day a week); explain precisely why it's justified (the reasons you deserve more money than others they may have hired, or that your children come home from school early on Fridays). If you have no justification for a demand, it may be unwise to make it. Again, keep in mind the inherent tension between being likable and explaining why you deserve more: Suggesting that you're especially valuable can make you sound arrogant if you haven't thought through how best to communicate the message.

Make it clear they can get you

People won't want to expend political or social capital to get approval for a strong or improved offer if they suspect that at the end of the day, you're still going to say, "No, thanks." Who wants to be the stalking horse for another company? If you intend to negotiate for a better package, make it clear that you're serious about working for this employer. Sometimes you get people to want you by explaining that *everybody* wants you. But the more strongly you play that hand, the more they may think that they're not going to get you anyway, so why bother jumping through hoops? If you're planning to mention all the options you have as leverage, you should balance that by saying why—or under what conditions—you would be happy to forgo those options and accept an offer.

Understand the person across the table

Companies don't negotiate; people do. And before you can influence the person sitting opposite you, you have to understand her. What are her interests and individual concerns? For example, negotiating with a prospective boss is very different from negotiating with an HR representative. You can perhaps afford to pepper the latter with questions regarding details of the offer, but you don't want to annoy someone who may become your manager with seemingly petty demands. On the flip side, HR may be responsible for hiring 10 people and therefore reluctant to break precedent, whereas the boss, who will benefit more directly from your joining the company, may go to bat for you with a special request.

Understand their constraints

They may like you. They may think you deserve everything you want. But they still may not give it to you. Why? Because they may have certain ironclad constraints, such as salary caps, that no amount of negotiation can loosen. Your job is to figure out where they're flexible and where they're not. If, for example, you're talking to a large company that's hiring 20 similar people at the same time, it probably can't give you a higher salary than everyone else. But it may be flexible on start dates, vacation time, and signing bonuses. On the other hand, if you're negotiating with a smaller company that has never hired someone in your role, there may be room to adjust the initial salary offer or job title but not other things. The better you understand the constraints, the more likely it is that you'll be able to propose options that solve both sides' problems.

Be prepared for tough questions

Many job candidates have been hit with difficult questions they were hoping not to face: Do you have any other offers? If we make you an offer tomorrow, will you say yes? Are we your top choice? If you're unprepared, you might say something inelegantly evasive or, worse, untrue. My advice is to never lie in a negotiation. It frequently comes back to harm you, but even if it doesn't, it's unethical. The other risk is that, faced with a tough question, you may try too hard to please and end up losing leverage. The point is this: You need to prepare for questions and issues that would put you on the defensive, make you feel uncomfortable, or expose your weaknesses. Your goal is to answer honestly without looking like an unattractive candidate—and without giving up too much bargaining power. If you have thought in advance about how to answer difficult questions, you probably won't forfeit one of those objectives.

Focus on the questioner's intent, not on the question

If, despite your preparation, someone comes at you from an angle you didn't expect, remember this simple rule: It's not the question that matters but the questioner's intent. Often the question is

Women Who Negotiate a Job Offer Are Penalized: An "I-We" Strategy Can Help

by Hannah Riley Bowles

In several studies, the social cost of negotiating for higher pay as part of a job offer has been found to be greater for women than it is for men. In other words, both men and women are less willing to work with a woman who has attempted to negotiate than with a woman who has not. Men can certainly overplay their hand and alienate negotiating counterparts. However, these studies show that it generally makes no difference whether a man chooses to negotiate or not (the willingness of hiring managers to work with him remain the same), while for a woman, navigating the terrain of likability in negotiations carries a certain amount of risk.

The results of this research are important to understand before criticizing women—or before a woman criticizes herself—for being reluctant to negotiate. Their reticence is based on an accurate reading of the environment. Women who dread negotiating may be intuiting—correctly—that asking for higher pay in a job negotiation would present a socially difficult situation for them.

So we shouldn't blame women for being wary of negotiation. But is there anything they can do about it? Thankfully, yes.

Negotiating *on behalf of someone else* is seen as appropriately feminine behavior. Research shows that women perform better (e.g., negotiate higher salaries) when their role is to advocate for others as opposed to themselves. Creating what's called a relational or an "I-We" account is, therefore, one tactic that can be effective. This strategy involves asking for what you want while signaling to your counterpart that you also understand their perspective. How does it work?

First, explain to your counterpart why—from *their* perspective—it's appropriate for you to be negotiating. Sheryl Sandberg says that in her discussions with Facebook, she told her potential employers, "Of course you realize that you're hiring me to run your deal team, so you want me to be a good negotiator." Sandberg justified negotiating as essential to the position she was applying for. If she didn't demonstrate her ability to negotiate, Facebook would be crazy to hire her. She calls this a "think personally, act communally" strategy.

Second, signal to your counterpart that you care about organizational relationships. After pointing out that Facebook should want her to be a good negotiator, Sandberg recounts saying, "This is the only time you and I will ever be on opposite sides of the table." In other words, "I am clear that we're on the same team here."

In experimental research testing evaluators' impressions of negotiating scripts, we found that using a relational account helped women get what they wanted *and* avoid social penalty. One successful test script was very similar to Sandberg's but was written for a more junior employee: "I don't know how typical it is for people at my level to negotiate, but I'm hopeful that you'll see my skill at negotiating as something important that I can bring to the job." (I'm not suggesting that women use these scripts word for word. Come up with an "I-We strategy" that makes sense in your particular situation and feels authentic to you.)

When the scripted explanation for why the woman was negotiating seemed legitimate, evaluators were more inclined to grant her salary request (as compared to when she was negotiating without that explanation). When her script communicated concern for organizational relationships, evaluators were more inclined to work with her. Indeed, there was no significant difference in the willingness to work with a female job applicant who negotiated using a relational account as compared to female applicants who did not negotiate at all.

Not every legitimate explanation for negotiating helped women. For instance, we tested multiple scripts for negotiating a pay raise based on an outside offer—some scripts even suggesting that the other offer had just dropped into the employee's lap. But in every case, the suggestion that the employee would leave the company if the offer were not matched seemed to undermine the impression that the employee cared about organizational relationships. As a result, evaluators reported being more willing to grant a woman with an outside offer a raise, but they were disinclined to work with her.

I acknowledge that this idea of using "relational accounts" offends some women. It makes them feel as though they're bending to unjust stereotypes or simply being inauthentic. I sympathize with that reaction. We were surprised during the research that it was so hard to reduce the effects of backlash against women who negotiate.

It is good advice for *any* negotiator, male or female, to ask for what they want in terms that their counterparts will perceive as legitimate and mutually beneficial. But for women it is especially helpful because it can mitigate the real-life social costs of self-advocacy. By sharing this research, I hope to shed light on this form of bias. Most people don't want to discriminate. With more self-awareness as negotiators and evaluators, we can work to close the gender gap.

Adapted from "Why Women Don't Negotiate Their Job Offers," posted on hbr.org on June 19, 2014.

challenging, but the questioner's intent is benign. An employer who asks whether you would immediately accept an offer tomorrow may simply be interested in knowing if you are genuinely excited about the job, not trying to box you into a corner. A question about whether you have other offers may be designed not to expose your weak alternatives but simply to learn what type of job search you're conducting and whether this company has a chance of getting you. If you don't like the question, don't assume the worst. Rather, answer in a way that addresses what you think is the intent, or ask for a clarification of the problem the interviewer is trying to solve. If you engage in a genuine conversation about what he's after, and show a willingness to help him resolve whatever issue he has, both of you will be better off.

Consider the whole deal

Sadly, to many people, "negotiating a job offer" and "negotiating a salary" are synonymous. But much of your satisfaction from the job will come from other factors you can negotiate—perhaps even more easily than salary. Don't get fixated on money. Focus on the value of the entire deal: responsibilities, location, travel, flexibility in work hours, opportunities for growth and promotion, perks, support for continued education, and so forth. Think not just about *how* you're willing to be rewarded but also *when*. You may decide to chart a course that pays less handsomely now but will put you in a stronger position later.

Negotiate multiple issues simultaneously, not serially

If someone makes you an offer and you're legitimately concerned about parts of it, you're usually better off proposing all your changes at once. Don't say, "The salary is a bit low. Could you do something about it?" and then, once she's worked on it, come back with "Thanks. Now here are two other things I'd like . . ." If you ask for only one thing initially, she may assume that getting it will make you ready to accept the offer (or at least to make a decision). If you keep saying "and one more thing . . . ," she is unlikely to remain in a generous or understanding mood. Furthermore, if you have more than one request, don't simply mention all the things you want—A, B, C, and D; also signal the relative importance of each to you. Otherwise, she may pick the two things you value least, because they're pretty easy to give you, and feel she's met you halfway. Then you'll have an offer that's not much better and a negotiating partner who thinks her job is done.

Don't negotiate just to negotiate

Resist the temptation to prove that you are a great negotiator. MBA students who have just taken a class on negotiation are plagued by this problem: They go bargaining berserk the first chance they get, which is with a prospective employer. My advice: If something is important to you, absolutely negotiate. But don't haggle over every little thing. Fighting to get just a bit more can rub people the wrong way—and can limit your ability to negotiate with the company later in your career, when it may matter more.

Think through the timing of offers

At the beginning of a job hunt, you often want to get at least one offer in order to feel secure. This is especially true for people finishing a degree program, when everyone is interviewing and some are celebrating early victories. Ironically, getting an early offer can be problematic: Once a company has made an offer, it will expect an answer reasonably soon. If you want to consider multiple jobs, it's useful to have all your offers arrive close together. So don't be afraid to slow down the process with one potential employer or to speed it up with another in order to have all your options laid out at one time. This, too, is a balancing act: If you pull back too much—or push too hard—a company may lose interest and hire someone else. But there are subtle ways to solve such problems. For example, if you want to delay an offer, you might ask for a later second- or third-round interview.

Avoid, ignore, or downplay ultimatums of any kind

People don't like being told "Do this or else." So avoid giving ultimatums. Sometimes we do so inadvertently—we're just trying to show strength, or we're frustrated, and it comes off the wrong way.

Your counterpart may do the same. My personal approach when at the receiving end of an ultimatum is to simply ignore it, because at some point the person who gave it might realize that it could scuttle the deal and will want to take it back. He can do that much more easily without losing face if it's never been discussed. If someone tells you, "We'll never do this," don't dwell on it or make her repeat it. Instead you might say, "I can see how that might be difficult, given where we are today. Perhaps we can talk about X, Y, and Z." Pretend the ultimatum was never given and keep her from becoming wedded to it. If it's real, she'll make that clear over time.

Remember, they're not out to get you
Tough salary negotiations or long delays in the confirmation of a formal offer can make it seem that potential employers have it in for you. But if you're far enough along in the process, these people like you and want to continue liking you. Unwillingness to move on a particular issue may simply reflect constraints that you don't fully appreciate. A delay in getting an offer letter may just mean that you're not the only concern the hiring manager has in life. Stay in touch, but be patient. And if you can't be patient, don't call up in frustration or anger; better to start by asking for a clarification on timing and whether there's anything you can do to help move things along.

Stay at the table
Remember: What's not negotiable today may be negotiable tomorrow. Over time, interests and constraints change. When someone says no, what he's saying is "No—given how I see the world today." A month later that same person may be able to do something he couldn't do before, whether it's extending an offer deadline or increasing your salary. Suppose a potential boss denies your request to work from home on Fridays. Maybe that's because he has no flexibility on the issue. But it's also possible that you haven't yet built up the trust required to make him feel comfortable with that arrangement. Six months in, you'll probably be in a better position to persuade him that you'll work conscientiously away from the office.

Be willing to continue the conversation and to encourage others to revisit issues that were left unaddressed or unresolved.

Maintain a sense of perspective

This is the final and most important point. You can negotiate like a pro and still lose out if the negotiation you're in is the wrong one. Ultimately, your satisfaction hinges less on getting the *negotiation* right and more on getting the *job* right. Experience and research demonstrate that the industry and function in which you choose to work, your career trajectory, and the day-to-day influences on you (such as bosses and coworkers) can be vastly more important to satisfaction than the particulars of an offer. These guidelines should help you negotiate effectively and get the offer you deserve, but they should come into play only after a thoughtful, holistic job hunt designed to ensure that the path you're choosing will lead you where you want to go.

Originally published in April 2014. Reprint R1404K

Getting to *Sí, Ja, Oui, Hai,* and *Da*

by Erin Meyer

TIM CARR, AN AMERICAN working for a defense company based in the midwestern United States, was about to enter a sensitive bargaining session with a high-level Saudi Arabian customer, but he wasn't particularly concerned. Carr was an experienced negotiator and was well-trained in basic principles: Separate the people from the problem. Define your BATNA (best alternative to a negotiated agreement) up front. Focus on interests, not positions. He'd been there, read that, and done the training.

The lengthy phone call to Saudi Arabia proceeded according to plan. Carr carefully steered the would-be customer to accept the deal, and it seemed he had reached his goal. "So let me just review," he said. "You've agreed that you will provide the supplies for next year's project and contact your counterpart at the energy office to get his approval. I will then send a letter. . . . Next you've said that you will. . . ." But when Carr finished his detailed description of who had agreed to what, he was greeted with silence. Finally a soft but firm voice said, "I told you I would do it. You think I don't keep my promises? That I'm not good on my word?"

That was the end of the discussion—and of the deal.

The many theories about negotiation may work perfectly when you're doing a deal with a company in your own country. But in today's globalized economy you could be negotiating a joint venture in China, an outsourcing agreement in India, or a supplier contract in Sweden. If so, you might find yourself working with very different norms of communication. What gets you to "yes" in one culture gets you to "no" in another. To be effective, a negotiator must have a sense of how his counterpart is reacting. Does she want to cooperate? Is she eager, frustrated, doubtful? If you take stock of subtle messages, you can adjust your own behavior accordingly. In an international negotiation, however, you may not have the contextual understanding to interpret your counterpart's communication—especially unspoken signals—accurately. In my work and research, I find that when managers from different parts of the world negotiate, they frequently misread such signals, reach erroneous conclusions, and act, as Tim Carr did, in ways that thwart their ultimate goals.

In the following pages, I draw on my work on cross-cultural management to identify five rules of thumb for negotiating with someone whose cultural style of communication differs from yours. The trick, as we will see, is to be aware of key negotiation signals and to adjust both your perceptions and your actions in order to get the best results.

1. Adapt the Way You Express Disagreement

In some cultures it's appropriate to say "I totally disagree" or to tell the other party he's wrong. This is seen as part of a normal, healthy discussion. A Russian student of mine told me, "In Russia we enter the negotiation ready for a great big debate. If your Russian counterpart tells you passionately that he completely disagrees with every point you have made, it's not a sign that things are starting poorly. On the contrary, it's an invitation to a lively discussion."

In other cultures the same behavior would provoke anger and possibly an irreconcilable breakdown of the relationship. An American manager named Sean Green, who had spent years negotiating partnerships in Mexico, told me that he quickly learned that if he wanted to make progress toward a deal, he needed to say things like "I do not quite understand your point" and "Please explain more why you think that." If he said, "I disagree with that," the discussions might shut down completely.

Idea in Brief

The Problem

In cross-border negotiations, managers often discover that perfectly rational deals fall apart when their counterparts make what seem to be unreasonable demands or don't respect their commitments.

Why It Happens

Each culture has its own communication norms, and over time you'll find that what gets you to "yes" in one culture may get you to "no" in another.

The Solution

You can reduce miscommunication by respecting these five rules of thumb:

1. Figure out how to express disagreement.

2. Recognize what emotional expressiveness signifies.

3. Learn how the other culture builds trust.

4. Avoid yes-or-no questions.

5. Beware of putting it in writing.

The key is to listen for verbal cues—specifically, what linguistics experts call "upgraders" and "downgraders." Upgraders are words you might use to strengthen your disagreement, such as "totally," "completely," "absolutely." Downgraders—such as "partially," "a little bit," "maybe"—soften the disagreement. Russians, the French, Germans, Israelis, and the Dutch use a lot of upgraders with disagreement. Mexicans, Thai, the Japanese, Peruvians, and Ghanaians use a lot of downgraders.

Try to understand upgraders and downgraders within their own cultural context. If a Peruvian you're negotiating with says he "disagrees a little," a serious problem may well be brewing. But if your German counterpart says he "completely disagrees," you may be on the verge of a highly enjoyable debate.

2. Know When to Bottle It Up or Let It All Pour Out

In some cultures it's common—and entirely appropriate—during negotiations to raise your voice when excited, laugh passionately, touch your counterpart on the arm, or even put a friendly arm around him. In other cultures such self-expression not only feels intrusive or surprising but may even demonstrate a lack of professionalism.

What makes international negotiations interesting (and compli-cated) is that people from some very emotionally expressive cul-tures—such as Brazil, Mexico, and Saudi Arabia—may also avoid open disagreement. (See the exhibit "Preparing to face your coun-terpart.") Mexicans tend to disagree softly yet express emotions openly. As a Mexican manager, Pedro Alvarez, says, "In Mexico we perceive emotional expressiveness as a sign of honesty. Yet we are highly sensitive to negative comments and offended easily. If you disagree with me too strongly, I would read that as a signal that you don't like me."

In other cultures—such as Denmark, Germany, and the Netherlands—open disagreement is seen as positive as long as

Preparing to face your counterpart

The map below sorts nationalities according to how confrontational and emo-tionally expressive they are. Although negotiators often believe that the two characteristics go hand in hand, that's not always the case.

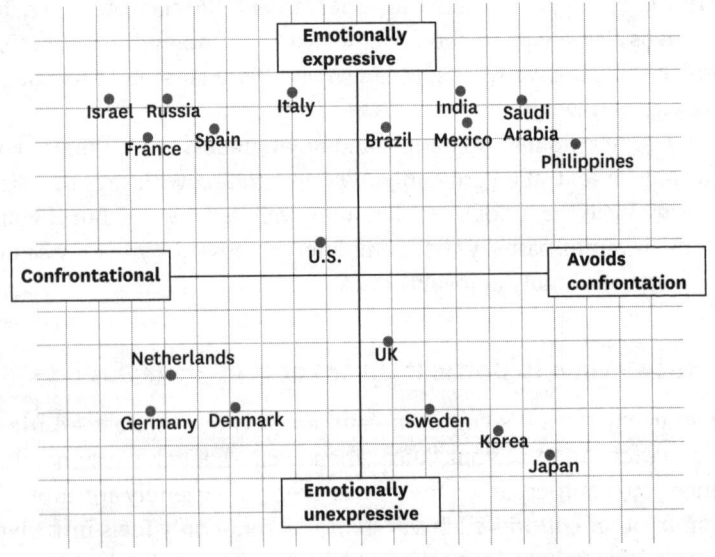

it is expressed calmly and factually. A German negotiator, Dirk Firnhaber, explains that the German word *Sachlichkeit,* most closely translated in English as "objectivity," refers to separating opinions from the person expressing them. If he says, "I totally disagree," he means to debate the opinions, not disapprove of the individual.

People from cultures like these may view emotional expressiveness as a lack of maturity or professionalism in a business context. Firnhaber tells a story about one deal he negotiated with a French company. It began calmly enough, but as the discussion continued, the French managers grew animated: "The more we discussed, the more our French colleagues became emotional—with voices raised, arms waving, ears turning red . . . the whole thing." Firnhaber was increasingly uncomfortable with the conversation and at times thought the deal would fall apart. To his surprise, the French took a very different view: "When the discussion was over, they seemed delighted with the meeting, and we all went out for a great dinner."

So the second rule of international negotiations is to recognize what an emotional outpouring (whether yours or theirs) signifies in the culture you are negotiating with, and to adapt your reaction accordingly. Was it a bad sign that the Swedish negotiators sat calmly across the table from you, never entered into open debate, and showed little passion during the discussion? Not at all. But if you encountered the same behavior while negotiating in Israel, it might be a sign that the deal was about to die an early death.

3. Learn How the Other Culture Builds Trust

During a negotiation, both parties are explicitly considering whether the deal will benefit their own business and implicitly trying to assess whether they can trust each other. Here cultural differences hit us hard. How we come to trust someone varies dramatically from one part of the world to another.

Consider this story from John Katz, an Australian negotiating a joint venture in China. Initially, he felt he was struggling to get the information his side needed, so he asked his company's China consultant for advice. The consultant suggested that Katz was going at the deal too quickly and should spend more time building trust. When Katz said he'd been working hard to do just that by supplying a lot of information from his side and answering all questions transparently, the consultant replied, "The problem is that you need to approach them from a relationship perspective, not a business perspective. You won't get what you want unless you develop trust differently."

Research in this area divides trust into two categories: *cognitive* and *affective.* Cognitive trust is based on the confidence you feel in someone's accomplishments, skills, and reliability. This trust comes from the head. In a negotiation it builds through the business interaction: You know your stuff. You are reliable, pleasant, and consistent. You demonstrate that your product or service is of high quality. I trust you. Affective trust arises from feelings of emotional closeness, empathy, or friendship. It comes from the heart. We laugh together, relax together, and see each other on a personal level, so I feel affection or empathy for you. I trust you.

In a business setting, the dominant type of trust varies dramatically from one part of the world to another. In one research project, Professor Roy Chua, of Singapore Management University, surveyed Chinese and American executives from a wide range of industries, asking them to list up to 24 important members of their professional networks. He then asked them to indicate the extent to which they felt comfortable sharing their personal problems and dreams with each of those contacts. "These items showed an affective-based willingness to depend on and be vulnerable to the other person," Chua explains. Finally, participants were asked to indicate how reliable, competent, and knowledgeable each contact was. These assessments showed a more cognitive-based willingness to depend on the other person.

The survey revealed that in negotiations (and business in general) Americans draw a sharp line between cognitive and affective trust. American culture has a long tradition of separating the emotional from the practical. Mixing the two risks conflict of interest and is viewed as unprofessional. Chinese managers, however, connect the two, and the interplay between cognitive and affective trust is much stronger. They are quite likely to develop personal bonds where they have financial or business ties.

In most emerging or newly emerged markets, from BRIC to Southeast Asia and Africa, negotiators are unlikely to trust their counterparts until an affective connection has been made. The same is true for most Middle Eastern and Mediterranean cultures. That may make negotiations challenging for task-oriented Americans, Australians, Brits, or Germans. Ricardo Bartolome, a Spanish manager, told me that he finds Americans to be very friendly on the surface, sometimes surprisingly so, but difficult to get to know at a deeper level. "During a negotiation they are so politically correct and careful not to show negative emotion," he said. "It makes it hard for us to trust them."

So in certain cultures you need to build an affective bond or emotional connection as early as possible. Invest time in meals and drinks (or tea, karaoke, golf, whatever it may be), and don't talk about the deal during these activities. Let your guard down and show your human side, including your weaknesses. Demonstrate genuine interest in the other party and make a friend. Be patient: In China, for example, this type of bond may take a long time to build. Eventually, you won't have just a friend; you'll have a deal.

4. Avoid Yes-or-No Questions

At some point during your negotiation you'll need to put a proposal on the table—and at that moment you will expect to hear whether or not the other side accepts. One of the most confounding aspects of international negotiations is that in some cultures the word "yes" may be used when the real meaning is no. In other cultures "no" is the most frequent knee-jerk response, but it often means "Let's discuss further." In either case, misunderstanding the message can lead to a waste of time or a muddled setback.

A recent negotiation between a Danish company and its Indonesian supplier provides a case in point. One of the Danish executives wanted reassurance that the Indonesians could meet the desired deadline, so he asked them directly if the date was feasible.

Look for Cultural Bridges

THERE'S NO SUBSTITUTE for learning all you can about the culture you will be negotiating with. But taking a cultural bridge—someone who is from the other culture, has a foot in both cultures, or, at the very least, knows the other culture intimately—to the negotiating table will give you a head start.

Of course, if one party doesn't speak English well, it's common to have the help of a translator; but a cultural bridge can make a huge impact even if no linguistic divide exists. During breaks in the negotiation, for example, you can ask this person to interpret what's going on between the lines.

The British executive Sarah Stevens was leading a U.S. team negotiating a deal in Japan. The Japanese parties all spoke English well, but three hours into the negotiation Stevens realized that her team was doing 90% of the talking, which worried her. She asked a colleague from her company's Japan office for advice. He explained that the Japanese often pause to think before speaking—and that they don't find silence uncomfortable the way Americans or the British do. He advised Stevens to adopt the Japanese approach: After asking a question, wait patiently and quietly for an answer. He also told her that the Japanese often make decisions in groups, so they might need to confer before giving an answer. If after a period of silence no clear answer had been given, Stevens might suggest a short break so that they could have a sidebar.

To his face they replied that it was, but a few days later they informed the company by e-mail that it was not. The Danish executive was aggrieved. "We'd already wasted weeks," he says. "Why didn't they tell us transparently during the meeting? We felt they had lied to us point-blank."

After hearing this story, I asked an Indonesian manager to explain what had happened. He told me that from an Indonesian perspective, it is rude to look someone you respect and like in the eye and say no to a request. "Instead we try to show 'no' with our body language or voice tone," he said. "Or perhaps we say, 'We will try our best.'" Signals like these are a way of saying "We would like to do what you want, but it is not possible." The interlocutor assumes that his counterpart will get the message and that both parties can then move on.

The problem can work the other way. The Indonesian manager went on to describe his experience negotiating with a French

In Japan, he said, it is common to iron out a lot of potential conflicts in one-on-one informal discussions before the formal group meeting, which is seen more as a place to put a stamp on decisions already made. This particular nugget came too late for that trip, but Stevens made sure the next time to enable informal discussions in advance. Thanks to her cultural bridge, she got the deal she had hoped for.

If your team has no obvious candidate for this role, look elsewhere in your company. But don't make the common mistake of thinking that someone who speaks the language and has a parent from the culture will necessarily make a good cultural bridge.

Consider this British manager of Korean origin: He looked Korean, had a Korean name, and spoke Korean with no accent, but he'd never lived or worked in Korea; his parents had moved to Britain as teenagers. His company asked him to help with an important negotiation in Korea, but once there, he quickly realized that his team would have been better off without him. Because he spoke the language so well, the Koreans assumed that he would behave like a Korean, so they took offense when he spoke to the wrong person in the room and when he confronted them too directly. As he observes, "If I hadn't looked or sounded Korean, they would have forgiven me for behaving badly."

company for the first time: "When I asked them if they could kindly do something, the word 'no' flew out of their mouths—and not just once but often more like a 'no-no-no-no,' which feels to us like we are being slapped repeatedly." He found out later that the French were actually happy to accede to his request; they had just wanted to debate it a bit before final agreement.

When you need to know whether your counterpart is willing to do something, but his answer to every question leaves you more confused than before, remember the fourth rule of cross-cultural negotiations: If possible, avoid posing a yes-or-no question. Rather than "Will you do this?" try "How long would it take you to get this done?" And when you do ask a yes-or-no question in Southeast Asia, Japan, or Korea (perhaps also in India or Latin America), engage all your senses and emotional antennae. Even if the response is affirmative, something may feel like no: an extra beat of silence, a strong sucking in of the breath, a muttered "I will try, but it will be difficult." If so, the deal is probably not sealed. You may well have more negotiations in front of you.

5. Be Careful About Putting It in Writing

American managers learn early on to repeat key messages frequently and recap a meeting in writing. "Tell them what you're going to tell them, tell them, and then tell them what you've told them" is one of the first communication lessons taught in the United States. In Northern Europe, too, clarity and repetition are the basis of effective negotiation.

But this good practice can all too often sour during negotiations in Africa or Asia. A woman from Burundi who was working for a Dutch company says, "In my culture, if we have a discussion on the phone and come to a verbal agreement, that would be enough for me. If you get off the phone and send me a written recap of the discussion, that would be a clear signal that you don't trust me." This, she says, repeatedly caused difficulty for her company's negotiators, who recapped each discussion in writing as a matter of both habit and principle.

The difference in approach can make it difficult to write a contract. Americans rely heavily on written contracts—more so than any other culture in the world. As soon as two parties have agreed on the price and details, long documents outlining what will happen if the deal is not kept, and requiring signatures, are exchanged. In the U.S. these contracts are legally binding and make it easy to do business with people we otherwise have no reason to trust.

But in countries where the legal system is traditionally less reliable, and relationships carry more weight in business, written contracts are less frequent. In these countries they are often a commitment to do business but may not be legally binding. Therefore they're less detailed and less important. As one Nigerian manager explains, "If the moment we come to an agreement, you pull out the contract and hand me a pen, I start to worry. Do you think I won't follow through? Are you trying to trap me?"

In Nigeria and many other high-growth markets where the business environment is rapidly evolving, such as China and Indonesia, successful businesspeople must be much more flexible than is necessary (or desirable) in the West. In these cultures, a contract marks the beginning of a relationship, but it is understood that as the situation changes, the details of the agreement will also change.

Consider the experience of John Wagner, an American who had been working out a deal with a Chinese supplier. After several days of tough negotiations, his team and its legal department drafted a contract that the Chinese seemed happy to sign. But about six weeks later they reopened discussion on points that the Americans thought had been set in stone. Wagner observes, "I see now that we appeared irrationally inflexible to them. But at the time, we were hitting our heads against our desks." For the Americans, the contract had closed the negotiation phase, and implementation would follow. But for the Chinese, signing the contract was just one step in the dance.

So the fifth and final rule for negotiating internationally is to proceed cautiously with the contract. Ask your counterparts to draft the first version so that you can discern how much detail they are planning to commit to before you plunk down a 20-page document for them to sign. And be ready to revisit. When negotiating in emerging markets, remember that everything in these countries is dynamic, and no deal is ever really 100% final.

Finally, don't forget the universal rules: When you are negotiating a deal, you need to persuade and react, to convince and finesse, pushing your points while working carefully toward an agreement. In the heat of the discussion, what is spoken is important. But the trust you have built, the subtle messages you have understood, your ability to adapt your demeanor to the context at hand, will ultimately make the difference between success and failure—for Americans, for Chinese, for Brazilians, for everybody.

Originally published in December 2015. Reprint R1512E

Negotiating Without a Net

A Conversation with the NYPD's Dominick J. Misino.
by Diane L. Coutu

NEGOTIATION INFORMS ALL ASPECTS of business life. Every interaction—with customers, with suppliers, and even with partners and investors—involves some kind of negotiation. In fact, in some languages the same term is used for both "business" and "negotiation." But the costs of failure can be high. The breakdown of negotiations between Hewlett-Packard's management and its founding families, for example, put the company's future in doubt and led to an expensive proxy fight.

Perhaps it's not surprising, then, that the last 20 years have seen an endless stream of handbooks on business negotiation, many of them best-sellers. Or that most of the country's top business schools have entire academic departments devoted to the subject. The advice is often helpful, even insightful. Who could argue with the recommendation that negotiators look for mutual gain and know their best alternative to a negotiated agreement? But you can't help feeling that the scholarly ink and classroom simulations of Negotiation 101 don't do enough to prepare businesspeople for the really tough negotiations—the ones where failure is not an option.

So where can you look for guidance? Since the 1970s, the New York Police Department has been training officers in hostage negotiation, arguably the highest-stake situation of all. Founded in 1972, in the year after the Attica State Prison riot, the NYPD program was the country's first such training program. Another year later, in the wake of the Munich Olympics hostage crisis, the FBI established its own program, which was modeled on the NYPD's. Today, most law enforcement agencies in this country and others provide some kind of negotiation training, as local and national law enforcement officials face bargaining with armed criminals, terrorists, and psychopaths as part of their daily reality.

To find out what businesspeople can learn about handling tough negotiations from the experience of law enforcement, HBR senior editor Diane L. Coutu visited former NYPD detective and hostage negotiator Dominick Misino at his home on Long Island, New York, in 2002. (Misino died in 2013.) A member of the force for 22 years, Misino received international acclaim in 1993 when he successfully persuaded the hijacker of Lufthansa Flight 592 to lay down his gun and turn himself in at Kennedy Airport. Misino spent the last six years of his career as a primary negotiator, handling more than 200 incidents and never losing a single life.

After retiring in 1995, he taught negotiating skills to law enforcement officials, military personnel, and business executives. Misino modestly described hostage negotiation as "applied common sense." In the following interview, edited for clarity and length, he explored what he meant by that innocuous-sounding term, painting a vivid picture of the blood, sweat, and tears of hostage negotiation.

What special skills does it take to be a crisis negotiator?

I don't think it requires special skills. Anyone can do it, man or woman, uniformed or civilian. What crisis negotiation does take is what I call applied common sense. When I'm negotiating, I'm constantly asking myself, "What is the simplest thing I can do to solve the problem?" When I'm dealing with an armed criminal, for example, my first rule of thumb is simply to be polite. This sounds trite, I know, but it is very important.

A lot of times, the people I'm dealing with are extremely nasty. And the reason for this is that their anxiety level is so high: A guy armed and barricaded in a bank is in a fight-or-flight mode. To defuse the situation, I've got to try to understand what's going on in

Idea in Brief

In some languages, the word for "business" is the same as the word for "negotiation." That's not really surprising: Every interaction—with customers, suppliers, and even partners and investors—entails negotiation. And some involve very high stakes: The breakdown in negotiations between Hewlett-Packard's management and its founding families, for instance, put the company's future in doubt.

Dominick Misino is a man who knows about negotiating when the stakes are at their very highest. As a hostage negotiator for the New York Police Department, Misino successfully persuaded the hijacker of Lufthansa Flight 592 to lay down his gun and turn himself in. Misino spent the last 6 years of his career as a primary negotiator, handling more than 200 incidents and never losing a life. Since his retirement in 1995, he has taught negotiating skills to law enforcement officials, military personnel, and business executives.

Anyone can become a crisis negotiator, Misino contends. It takes what he calls "applied common sense." Be polite. Listen. Acknowledge the other guy's point of view (no matter what it is). But it's clear that in dealing with hijackers, kidnappers, and child molesters, Misino is far from passive. Negotiation, he says, is really a series of small agreements, and he is adept at orchestrating those agreements from the start so that his adversary learns to trust him and come around to his point of view.

In vivid and sometimes hair-raising detail, Misino demonstrates how he gets criminals to trust police officers enough to refrain from harming innocent parties and give themselves up. Many of the techniques he describes are surprisingly applicable to business negotiations, where the parties may seem equally intractable and failure is not an option.

his head. The first step to getting there is to show him respect, which shows my sincerity and reliability. So before the bad guy demands anything, I always ask him if he needs something. Obviously I'm not going to get him a car. I'm not going to let him go. But it makes excellent sense to be sensitive to the other guy's needs. When you give somebody a little something, he feels obligated to give you something back. That's just good common sense.

Don't you find it difficult to be polite to a murderer or a rapist?

I'll go even further. How do you show respect to a convicted child molester? Believe me, in my line of work we routinely deal with people who have moved out of society and done things that are just horrific. Obviously, it isn't easy to negotiate with someone you dislike—but if you're a professional, you keep your feelings separate from your work.

In crisis negotiation, you have the advantage that your goal is constantly right in front of your face: Get everybody out alive. And you're also under incredible time pressure. When an Ethiopian national hijacked that Lufthansa plane, I had less than 45 minutes to build a relationship with him and bring the plane down. There were 104 people on board, and the hijacker had a gun aimed at the pilot's head. That's all the motivation I needed to stay focused on my task. Of course, there are people—whole countries, even—who say that we should never negotiate with certain individuals—terrorists, for instance. But I think that's extreme. In reality, we're always ready to negotiate as hard as we can with anyone to show him that there is an alternative to violence. Of course, we're also ready to come in with a tactical solution—to deploy the SWAT teams—if we have to. But, ideally, force is a last resort.

Can you give other examples of what you mean by applied common sense?

Another very commonsense technique is to ask the bad guy very early on in a negotiation if he wants you to tell him the truth. I stumbled on this tactic when I first started negotiating. My backup team found out that the bad guy had been part of a street gang. So I said, "Look, you grew up on the streets. So did I. Do you want me to lie to you or tell the truth?" And he said he wanted the truth, which, of course, is exactly what I expected him to say. His situation was desperate; there were snipers all over the place. Who in his right mind would have wanted to be lied to?

The critical thing you get by asking the other guy if he wants the truth is that he enters into an agreement with you right at the start. This is important because a successful negotiation is really a series of small agreements. You use every possible opportunity to agree with your adversary—and to get him to agree with you. Because all the while you're agreeing, the other guy is learning that he can trust you, that nobody's going to hurt him. So I try right away to get to the first yes, and then immediately I go for the second. I tell the bad guy that if he wants me to tell him the truth, then he might hear things he doesn't want to hear and, if that happens, he's got to agree not to hurt anybody. In my day, I've negotiated with hostage-takers, hijackers, and murderers; the majority of them have given me their word they won't hurt anyone. These people may be the outcasts of society, but they do have a code of honor. In fact, I would say that over 90% of the times that a criminal has given me his promise, he has kept it.

If you don't have to learn special skills, do you need certain personal qualities to be a successful high-stakes negotiator?

On the most basic level, you have to be a good listener. Unfortunately, like most people, negotiators want to talk and be heard, and so they've got to learn how to let the other person express himself without interruption. That's terribly important because the individuals with whom we are dealing are often the very people who have never been listened to, and they are desperate to be heard. They just don't have the patience for you to butt in and make a mistake. To get around this, I try to be a very active listener. For example, I typically ask the other guy to tell me his side of things. And then I sit back and get an earful. I hear every instance of when the other guy has ever been wronged. I find out how often he's been framed. I discover how no one has ever cared for him. And a lot of this is true. But the way I look at it is that all of it is true—to him. And that's what matters.

So top negotiators are excellent listeners. But they also need to be aware of the noise inside their own heads. Believe me, even if you don't know what's going on inside you, the other guy will. Their sensitivity to your own biases is extraordinary. You need to know your hot buttons and your limitations.

Personally, I've got a lot of trouble dealing with pederasts and other people who harm children. But nevertheless I can negotiate with these people because I'm aware of my feelings. I would even say my feelings push me to become a better negotiator because when I know that something is going to affect me, I work harder to achieve a level of objectivity. That's all part of being comfortable with who you are, which is essential for being able to negotiate. Take police negotiations: They are impromptu and can go on for 50 minutes or ten hours; nobody knows. The only thing for certain is that no one can sustain a facade under that kind of pressure for very long. So the best preparation in the world for a successful negotiation is just to be comfortable with yourself.

Your reference to active listening sounds very reminiscent of what psychoanalysts call empathic listening. Can you say more?

Almost by definition, crisis negotiation is a roller coaster of emotions, both yours and the other guy's. To me, active listening means being attuned to those emotions, identifying them, and helping the other guy to work them through. One of the most effective ways of doing this is by a technique we call mirroring. We echo the other guy's remarks to try and build a bridge between us. For example, I'll say, "So, you have a gun."

And typically the bad guy says, "Yeah, I have a gun."

"A gun?" I repeat.

"Yeah," he says, "a nine-millimeter gun."

And so I echo him again: "nine-millimeter?"

"Yeah, nine-millimeter with two magazines, 18 rounds."

In this exchange, of course, I'm getting critical data. But at the same time I'm telling the bad guy that there is no longer a gun separating him and me; instead, there is some vital piece of information that the two of us share. In this way, mirroring is the beginning of a real conversation.

Another active-listening technique is to be constantly on the alert for the feelings being expressed behind the words. This is not as obvious as it sounds. My former partner once had an elderly woman who had barricaded herself in a house with a ten-inch butcher knife, and she was cursing at him at the top of her lungs. Despite her profanity, my partner was able to detect something else. He said to her, "Martha, I can hear your pain. I hear it in your voice." And she went from ranting and raving to absolute silence. No one before had ever picked up on the fact that she was hurting so much. When my partner acknowledged her pain, she put down the butcher knife, and he could begin to treat her like the elderly grandmother she was.

It sounds hokey until you've experienced it, but the very act of listening is empathetic. And when we do talk, we try to reinforce the empathy by using a lot of "we" statements: "We're in this together" or "We can work this out." This is the kind of language that can alleviate the bad guy's isolation and paranoia.

It sounds as if you're trying to put yourself in the other guy's shoes. Is that right?

Up to a point, but you've got to be careful about telling a hijacker or a rapist that you know exactly what he's going through, because usually you don't. In fact, you can really infuriate people by trying to identify with them, because they know that you know very little about what they've been through in their lives. One time, one of our guys tried to commiserate with a bad guy, and the guy just went ballistic. He started cursing and screaming: "When was the last time *you* ever held up a bank and took five hostages?" So putting yourself in the other guy's shoes isn't always as helpful as it sounds. In fact, I've often been struck in my own negotiations by how impossible it is for me to imagine the amount of stress a bad guy feels when he's holed up in a building with 100 heavily armed SWAT team officers focused on him, watching his every move. Truthfully, I have probably never felt as scared or angry or lonely in my entire life as that guy does at that moment.

You've talked about good negotiators; what makes a bad one?

The worst negotiators are the people who hate rejection. Of course, nobody likes rejection—it hurts your feelings. But bad negotiators can't accept the fact that all the negative stuff coming at them is not personal. They think the other guy is angry at them when the other guy doesn't even know them. I used to get yelled at all the time in my job, but as I tell my students, you just have to let the other person vent. Because if you do, there's an incredible payoff.

First of all, the other guy usually feels better. But even more important, in the process of letting off steam, the bad guy is likely to tell you his problem—and the solution to his problem. For instance, I once heard a bad guy ranting and raving because a negotiator was Italian. That helped us figure out pretty quickly that the negotiator had to go. But generally speaking, bad negotiators lack this perspective. They get their feelings hurt, which makes them soft—or defensive. Both are bad positions from which to negotiate.

So the other guy needs to vent. What about you?

Certainly you experience a lot of negative emotions in this job. You feel rage and frustration; you are almost always scared. I once participated in a negotiation that went on for 12 hours, though I wasn't the prime negotiator all that time. The most frustrating part was that the guy refused to talk. He just wouldn't talk. I have a tape recording of the negotiation, and whenever I hear it again, I realize how totally pent up I was feeling. I think if I could have reached out and strangled that guy, I probably would have.

There's nothing wrong with having strong emotions during a negotiation, but you need to acknowledge them so you don't act them out. That's the rule of thumb. But even here there are some exceptions. The most aggressive thing I've ever said in a negotiation situation was to a burglar who was threatening to kill his hostage, an 84-year-old lady named Ruth. As his threats grew more intense, I felt rage coming up inside me. And I said to the guy, "If you touch a hair on her head, I will personally ID your body in the morgue." Now, threatening your hostage-taker is not a suggested negotiation tactic. But in this situation, my gut told me that if I sat there all day listening to this particular guy threaten this particular lady, he was going to kill her. So I had to intervene. I did, and instantly the criminal backed down.

That was the only time I ever threatened a criminal in this way, but at the same time I must admit that I do not believe the best negotiators *never* act on their feelings. I think if you don't find yourself taking some risks in this job—if you don't find yourself going someplace you never intended on going—then you probably aren't being the best negotiator you can be.

It seems that you have to put a lid on some strong feelings. What helps you do that?

Having a team behind you is essential. Back in the early days, there were no negotiation teams. Negotiators worked one-on-one, and the stress was extraordinary. The longest consecutive negotiation I ever did was nine hours, and that was like running the New York City marathon. I just can't imagine how anyone could survive an ordeal like that without team support.

Nowadays, most police negotiation teams consist of five people. There is the primary negotiator, who actually talks to the bad guy. Then there is the commander, who makes all the decisions, and the coach who provides moral support and backup. These are the primary players. There's also a gopher or float, who runs around gathering vital information, and a guy we call a scribe. He keeps a chronological log of all the important stuff that's going on during the negotiation. It sounds crazy, but one of the things you often forget in the heat of a hostage situation is the other guy's name. So the scribe writes that down in big black letters on a piece of paper, which he tapes to the wall of the house or apartment we're negotiating out of.

An important point about these teams is that they're deliberately set up to separate negotiation from decision making, which gives the primary negotiator both terrific relief and enormous power to negotiate. Imagine for a moment that you're negotiating, and you tell the bad guy that you're in charge. He responds by demanding a car in 30 minutes or he'll take out a hostage. If, on the other hand, you can say, "Look, my commander is in charge, and I have to consult him," you've bought yourself time to maneuver.

This is the way diplomats operate all the time. They work out a proposal and then bring it back to the national leaders for approval. Of course, in a crisis situation you don't have days and months to discuss a proposal. You don't even have minutes. You come to a fork in the road, and you have fractions of seconds to decide whether to go right or left. This kind of pressure would be unendurable without a team's direction.

I guess that a lot of the time you didn't meet the people you were dealing with face-to-face. Was that a problem?

I hate to say it, but face-to-face communication is very old-fashioned. We rarely do that nowadays. Originally, the NYPD agreed with the communication gurus who said that face-to-face negotiation creates more intimacy and trust. But we quickly found out that face-to-face communication with a psychopath or an armed criminal is highly dangerous. In fact, the only police negotiators who have ever been killed in a negotiation situation were those who had face-to-face contact. So we dropped the approach altogether except for those situations in which there is absolutely no other way.

Normally, we prefer to work with the other guy by phone. Either we tap a phone line or drop a phone into the barricaded zone. However we manage it, phone contact is extremely effective. Americans are totally comfortable with the phone. We argue on the phone; we drive and talk on the phone; I've even heard of people who do therapy on the phone. Ironically, in my experience, the bad guys are often more comfortable on the phone than in face-to-face contact because they feel safer being at some distance from the police. If they're standing in the same room with you, they feel more exposed.

There is another reason we don't communicate face-to-face. We don't want to have the other guy see the inner machinations of our team. Think about what the scribe does, for example. If by some chance the bad guy would even surmise that someone is writing down information about him, he might not just feel insulted; he might feel threatened. After all, if you have someone who's barricaded or holding hostages, he's going to be highly paranoid about his safety.

What's the most dangerous negotiation situation?

Generally speaking, suicide is the most dangerous situation because it's the most volatile. There's no suffering for people who are threatening suicide. By the time they get this far, they have finished suffering. So unlike criminals who are facing a jail term, suicidal people fear nothing. They're not worried that they might be punished for what they're doing to themselves—or to you. They're just not thinking. And, as we've seen with the suicide bombers in Israel, that makes them some of the most dangerous people we could ever deal with.

Once I had a suicidal ex–police officer who had climbed to the top of the Whitestone Bridge. A lot of people who saw her said, "Aw, she's up there just because she wants the publicity." But I never believed that. It was clear to me that she had emotional problems. Her therapist came to the scene after I had talked her down, and he told the team that we had handled her perfectly because we under-stood intuitively how dangerous she was. In fact, he told us, she was not only suicidal; she was homicidal. "She wouldn't have hesitated, if you made her mad, to grab one of you and take you over the bridge with her." Incidentally, suicide is the main reason we never allow a priest or a rabbi to talk to a bad guy. We have learned over and over that when people ask for clergy, they are virtually always looking for closure on their lives. It's a prelude to suicide.

What's the biggest lesson you have learned from your work as a crisis negotiator?

I don't know if it's the biggest lesson, but one very important thing you learn as a negotiator is that if you want to win, you have to help the other guy to save face. Look at the people I deal with. They're criminals. They're not book-learned. Yet they're very smart in the sense that they can survive in an environment where most of us cannot, and they also have their own kind of dignity. If you can show these guys a way to maintain their pride while facing a defeat they know is inevitable, they'll go along with what you want.

I learned that lesson early in my negotiation career when I was called in to deal with a situation in Spanish Harlem. It was a hot sum-mer night, and there were 300 or 400 people out on the streets at three o'clock in the morning. A young man with a loaded shotgun had blockaded himself inside a crowded tenement building. He told me he wanted to surrender but couldn't because he'd look weak.

Now this guy was a parole violator, not a murderer, and so I told him that if he calmed down and let me cuff him, I would make it look as if I had to use force. He put down his gun and behaved like a perfect gentleman until we got to the street, where he started screaming like crazy and raising hell, as we had agreed. While he was doing this, the crowd was chanting "José! José!" in wild approval, and we threw him into the back of the car, jumped on the gas, and sped off. Two blocks later, José sat up, broke into a huge grin, and said to me, "Hey man, thank you. I really appreciated that." He recognized that I had given him a way out that didn't involve killing people and being killed in turn. I've never forgotten that.

Originally published in October 2002. Reprint R0210C

Deal Making 2.0

A guide to complex negotiations. *by David A. Lax and James K. Sebenius*

MOST BIG DEALS are built on a series of smaller ones. That's true of megamergers, major sales, infrastructure projects, and even some UN resolutions. These deals are the culmination of many focused negotiations among various parties, each with its own concerns. Most deal-making advice addresses how to choose the right tactics for each piece of the puzzle. Absent from the literature is guidance on how best to put the pieces together, let alone how to identify them in the first place. This leaves a glaring gap.

Consider the case of Mittal Steel's takeover of Arcelor, Europe's largest steel company—an intricate deal ultimately worth $33.1 billion. Suppose that founder Lakshmi Mittal had simply set up a meeting with Arcelor's chief executive to hammer out an acquisition. However persuasive Mittal's pitch, Arcelor would have rebuffed it; indeed, the company's board and CEO were, according to numerous accounts, dead set against the sale at first. Instead, Mittal and his son Aditya, the firm's CFO, undertook what we call a "negotiation campaign" involving multiple financial agreements; extensive shareholder and political dealings in Luxembourg, France, the Netherlands, and Canada; and regulatory accords in Brussels and Washington. These separate negotiations allowed Mittal to build sufficient support to overcome and even convert potential blockers.

The Mittal deal involved high stakes, but many small-scale deals play out on multiple fronts as well. The champion of a new product, for instance, has to orchestrate complex internal negotiations across individuals and departments in order to secure support and senior executive approval. Founders of a new venture must weave a web of mutually reinforcing deals: raising money on the right terms from the right sources, persuading credible figures to join the board, forging agreements with critical employees, working out contracts with strategic partners, and so on.

Each component deal in these situations presents a *tactical* challenge "at the table." This kind of direct negotiation is familiar terrain to deal makers. Less familiar is how to address the more *strategic* challenge that unfolds away from the table: sequencing the individual component deals in a way that allocates scarce negotiation efforts toward achieving the target outcome with enough support to make it stick. We have come to think of the process as a campaign, frequently conducted on multiple fronts, each typically involving many parties. On the basis of our analysis of and experience advising dozens of complex deals—and drawing on insights from sales, marketing, political, and even military campaigns—we have developed concepts and tools to help executives conduct such campaigns. In this article, we lay out the process, offering advice on how to identify the relevant parties, define and sequence the fronts, and orchestrate the complex set of deals that build a winning coalition.

But first, to illustrate what we mean by a multifront campaign—and the limitations of direct negotiation—we'll describe what happened when port operators on the U.S. Pacific coast faced the longshoremen from a position of weakness. (The story draws on various sources, especially a Harvard Business School case written by Kathleen McGinn and Dina Witter.) While labor disputes such as this can be politically polarizing, the Pacific Maritime Association's multifront approach incorporated many useful principles for overcoming daunting barriers and negotiating agreements that can ultimately be beneficial for all parties.

Idea in Brief

Direct negotiation "at the table" often makes sense. But for complex deals, which are usually built on a series of smaller ones involving multiple parties, a more strategic approach is to focus on what unfolds away from the table: the process of sequencing individual deals in a way that achieves the target outcome with enough support to make it stick.

A "negotiation campaign," which may take months or even years, involves identifying the relevant parties and grouping them into fronts; determining if the fronts can be combined; figuring out the order in which you will engage the fronts; and assessing how much information to share among the parties—and with your opponents.

When Boeing set out to sell $11 billion worth of aircraft to Air India, in late 2005, the company did significant advance work to build support for the deal on many fronts: its internal departments; banks, export agencies, and aircraft leasing companies; and the Indian government, which holds an ownership stake in the airline.

Showdown on the Waterfront

The Pacific Maritime Association (PMA) represents 72 U.S. and global shipping lines, including the behemoths Maersk and Hanjin, along with terminal operators in ports from San Diego to Seattle. The organization traditionally held contract negotiations every three years with the International Longshore and Warehouse Union (ILWU). When Joseph Miniace became the PMA's president, his priority for the 1999 talks was an agreement to introduce new information technologies that would help overcome the paralyzing inefficiencies of clogged West Coast ports.

At the bargaining table, however, Miniace's efforts crashed into potent union opposition to anything that might lead to future job loss, even if the agreement guaranteed current jobs. This pushback from organized labor was understandable: Containerization and other technological changes had slashed the ILWU's West Coast ranks by roughly 90% since the 1950s.

Wielding its power over U.S. seaborne trade flowing through the West Coast—then worth some $6 billion a week—the union began an informal slowdown. Loaded container ships soon backed up in harbors, disrupting supply chains. Pressure on the PMA (and the union) to make a deal came from companies such as Walmart, Dell, Home Depot, Nissan, and Boeing (which all depended on ocean shipping for parts and products), from agricultural interests whose produce would quickly spoil, and from the government. The PMA, a fragmented organization of both huge and minor shipping players, quickly caved.

Looking ahead to the 2002 contract talks, Miniace was resolved to reintroduce technology issues in order to address port congestion, which was only getting worse. But he worried about the ILWU's response. As labor expert Howard Kimeldorf has said, "In terms of economic muscle, [the ILWU] may be the strongest union in the country." Its members' compensation reflected the long-term results of this bargaining power: By 2002 annual wages for union members, including overtime, averaged $83,000 for longshoremen, $118,000 for clerks, and $158,000 for foremen.

Pause for a moment to consider the negotiating advice you would offer Miniace. Standard suggestions might include active listening, persuasion, trust building, putting oneself in the other party's shoes, starting with no, deciphering body language, inventing win-win options, and locking 'em in a room until they agree. While effective in many situations, such tactics would prove pathetically inadequate in the face of the ILWU's credible threat to shut down $6 billion worth of U.S. foreign trade a week.

So this time Miniace took a different approach to boosting the PMA's weak position. Well in advance of the 2002 talks, he embarked on a four-front campaign. Its effect was to set the stage so that the longshoremen would ultimately view a "yes" to Miniace's technology proposal as better than a "no."

Front 1: Internal

Miniace focused on his own organization first, visiting and patiently educating the PMA's shipping-firm members on the importance of new technologies and sometimes bringing pressure from major retailers and manufacturers. Thus armed, Miniace got PMA agreement to restructure and shrink its board to include fewer labor relations executives, who were invested in smooth contract negotiations, and more operating executives, who were focused on the economic consequences of repeated concessions. The PMA also agreed to change the board's decision-making procedures, moving from a consensus model to a voting model in which votes would be weighted according to shipping tonnage. Thus the biggest players would have the most influence.

Front 2: Business

Miniace then coordinated closely with Robin Lanier, who had built many close ties as the president of the International Mass Retail Association. She brought the case to shippers, large importers, manufacturers, and retailers such as Walmart, whose input had been helpful on the internal PMA front. Those parties had a natural, though previously untapped, interest in the negotiations—the new technology would reduce total shipping time and permit more-accurate cargo tracking—so they were eager to press for measures to increase the efficiency of port operations.

Front 3: Government

Next, Miniace and his team arranged visits to the U.S. departments of commerce, treasury, labor, transportation, and homeland security, and to the Office of the United States Trade Representative. He did not ask for favors. Rather, he pointed out how severe the economic impact of the 1999 union slowdown had been. In the event of a similar move by the ILWU, he said, the PMA would not settle. Instead, it would shut down the ports.

Front 4: The public

Finally, the PMA took the public relations initiative to frame its message to the media and the wider public. This involved painting a picture of a privileged, well-paid, antitechnology union.

A restructured board, energized business and political allies, and a targeted PR initiative put the PMA in a far stronger position. During the talks, the union initiated another slowdown, and the

PMA responded with the promised port shutdown. President George W. Bush believed he had sufficient backing to invoke the emergency provisions of the Taft-Hartley Act—the federal law governing the activities of labor unions—for the first time in more than 30 years. This forced both parties back to work, effectively blunting the ILWU's weapon and raising the cost of saying no.

Old-school tales of labor negotiations often emphasize table-pounding principals locked in a room until they reach a deal. New-age versions emphasize trust building and careful listening. Here, Miniace's away-from-the-table, sequential campaign on several fronts made the difference. As the lead union negotiator ruefully observed, "It used to be that the negotiation took place at the table."

The PMA's campaign was a forceful one, but the organization tried to avoid a purely coercive approach since the parties would have to live together. Ultimately, with the assistance of federal mediators, the parties negotiated a mutually beneficial agreement that gave technology rights to the shippers and jurisdiction over new technology jobs to union members, and guaranteed current union jobs. In an unprecedented affirmation of the new deal, the two sides agreed to a six-year rather than a three-year term. The PMA and the ILWU uneventfully negotiated another six-year deal in 2008. By 2010 both employment and tonnage through West Coast ports had shot up from 2002 levels by almost 40%.

When and Why to Choose a Campaign

When is a campaign likely to be more effective than direct negotiation? To answer that question, you need to identify your target outcome and then assess any barriers that stand in your way. These often include negotiation weakness (for instance, you have a poor no-deal option, but the other side can walk away without losing much), too little value in the deal, and opponents who could block an agreement.

How would a campaign help overcome the barriers you've identified? Would it make your desired outcome more likely by building up useful alliances, enhancing your credibility, increasing the value you bring to the table, strengthening your no-deal option, weakening that of the other side, or thwarting potential blockers? Will you need to negotiate approvals or buy-in—say, securing key contracts or distribution rights—before you even reach the main table? If the answer to any of those questions is yes, proceed with a campaign. In the PMA case, it was time for a different approach: Replaying the failed direct negotiation of 1999 in the 2002 talks without shoring up the shippers' weak position would probably have led to the same poor outcome, because the same high barriers would have stood in the way.

Designing and Executing a Campaign

There are six steps to reaching your target deal—and building a winning coalition that can make it stick.

1. Choose the right parties and group them into fronts

Given the barriers to agreement that you've identified, what parties must—or could usefully—be involved, and how should you group them into more-manageable fronts? In some cases, the answers are reasonably clear. Consider Boeing's campaign to sell $11 billion worth of 787 Dreamliners and other planes to Air India in late 2005. To succeed, Boeing needed to negotiate support from internal divisions and executives; strike deals with banks, export promotion agencies, and aircraft leasing companies; and reach agreements with the Indian government—which has an ownership stake in the airline—on the sourcing of domestic content from Indian manufacturers and the creation of local maintenance and pilot training organizations. Thus Boeing's campaign had to orchestrate negotiations on internal corporate fronts, external financial fronts, and political and national fronts.

But identifying parties and fronts isn't always so straightforward. As with the PMA campaign, the useful players may not be obvious at the outset. In Miniace's 1999 talks, he made the conventional assumption about whom to involve: his party and the one on the other side of the table. Yet figuring out the most advantageous set of parties for the 2002 talks—retailers, manufacturers, agricultural interests, federal agencies, and the broader public, as well as PMA

Finding the Right Parties for a Chinese Campaign

FOR DECADES, HONG KONG & CHINA Gas Company (HKCG) supplied-piped gas to Hong Kong's apartments and businesses.

In 2001 the company decided on a long-term growth strategy to take over the natural-gas-distribution systems in select mainland Chinese cities, upgrade them, and run them more efficiently.

This required HKCG to undertake challenging joint venture negotiations with multiple government agencies and other parties as well as with the entrenched managers of existing Chinese gas-distribution systems. These managers enjoyed considerable local power and opposed allowing "outsiders" to run the system.

To overcome these barriers, HKCG's managing director, Alfred Chan, and his team undertook lengthy multifront negotiation campaigns that involved patiently testing the waters with potential Chinese partners and getting clearance from local governments to establish joint ventures. But it wasn't always obvious which parties to target. As Chan describes it, "Almost 50% of our time and effort was spent gaining an understanding of the market (the

members—required creativity and initiative. (The sidebar "Finding the Right Parties for a Chinese Campaign" describes the disciplined process by which the Hong Kong & China Gas Company identified the welter of parties necessary to negotiate its many mainland-Chinese joint ventures.)

"Mapping backward" from your target deal is a useful tool for discovering who must be involved—or could be of use. So, for instance, you could consider your target's major influencers. If you're negotiating with a politician, you might want to reach major donors. If you're dealing with a CEO, you could look to big customers. You'll also want to seek out potential allies who can provide useful resources or information, players who might present credible alternatives to your target deal, and so on. Probe each party's interests and perceptions, key formal and informal relationships, and constituencies, and no-deal options. (Our previous HBR articles, "Six Habits of Merely Effective Negotiators" and "3-D Negotiation: Playing the Whole Game," offer more tools for this type of analysis.)

city where we hoped to operate), stakeholders (various city and provincial government officials), and other parties such as lawyers and bureaucrats."

What HKCG came to call its "social mapping" process often involved befriending lower-level target company personnel and using fee-requesting intermediaries—once Chan and his team could determine who was genuinely connected. As an HKCG employee observed, "Whom could we trust and who really mattered to the decision? It was never obvious from the company's organization chart; we had to figure it out. . . . In China, you are always dealing with the people and not just the project."

Several years into this new strategy, HKCG had completed more than 80 mainland joint ventures. "While negotiating the first several, we tended to think of the project planning, engineering, and financing aspects as the real challenges," one employee recalls. "As we gained more experience, however, we often found that negotiating the 'people' side of the equation was often the most difficult and the most critical factor for success."

You'll then want to determine if and how to group the parties. As with the Boeing–Air India case, a front may comprise groups that are of a similar kind or class or from like sectors or locations (bank debt holders, for example, or Brussels regulators). They may be organizationally related (staffs from government agencies or corporate units of a target acquisition). They may share key interests or maintain tight relationships (environmental NGOs or members of a family that has a controlling corporate interest). Although a front can consist of a single (important) party, it will more often be a collection of parties that can be grouped according to a common interest or affiliation.

2. Assess interdependencies among fronts

Are the fronts you've assembled largely independent, or can they positively or negatively affect one another? For example, is provisional agreement at both corporate and political levels helpful for financial negotiations? If a potential ally or blocker becomes aware of your activities on another front, will it help or hurt your overall prospects? If you deploy negotiating resources on one front, will that limit what you can deploy elsewhere? And so on.

3. Determine whether and when to combine fronts

In complex situations with a large number of fronts, dealing separately with each one may be an effective way to organize your team's efforts. But it may make sense to keep fronts separate only at the outset and combine them once you've made sufficient progress on each.

Combining fronts may generate gains from "package deals," in which success on a single front yields a resource (such as capital, intellectual property, a valuable customer, a powerful ally) that is worth most when combined with other, similar resources.

At the same time, combining fronts can inadvertently unite your opponents. When Conoco tried to establish consensus over building a pipeline in Ecuador's Amazon region, it negotiated on several fronts. One was composed of Ecuadorean and international advocates for indigenous peoples; another consisted of environmental NGOs. Both opposed Conoco's plans but mainly acted independently. However, when Conoco arranged a "consensus seeking" meeting of all stakeholders in a floating hotel on a river in the Amazon, the two groups combined forces in even more formidable opposition to Conoco, which ultimately withdrew from the project.

By contrast, in the late 1990s U.S. trade representative Charlene Barshefsky made a point of scheduling joint events for music, film, and software industry reps—who had traditionally operated independently—in order to unite the formerly separate players as allies behind her push for intellectual property negotiations with China.

In general, keep fronts separate when there is little or no interdependence among them, when there has not been sufficient progress on each, when they might negatively affect one another, or when joining them might create an opposing bloc. Combine fronts when it's important for transparency, when success on separate fronts can yield joint gains, and when doing so unites your allies. Timing is key, because progress on one front may help set up progress on the next. In the shippers-longshoremen case, for example, gaining the support of important business players greatly strengthened the PMA's hand as it sought the backing of government agencies and the president.

4. Sequence your campaign

Just as knowing which parties to approach in what order *within* a front can make or break a deal, so can smart sequencing *among* fronts. When the probability or value of success on one front is greatly enhanced by success elsewhere, focus elsewhere first. If a deal with a critical partner is conditional on your having locked in financing, for instance, concentrate first on the financial front.

Proper sequencing may also send important signals. Lining up a highly reputed lead investor, a well-regarded anchor tenant, or a big-name donor early in your campaign greatly increases the likelihood that other investors, satellite tenants, or smaller donors will come on board quickly and on favorable terms. Again, mapping backward is useful. In the run-up to the make-or-break congressional vote on the North American Free Trade Agreement, news would arrive in the office of Bill Daley, President Bill Clinton's key strategist on the pact, that a member of Congress who had been leaning toward yes had come out as a no. Daley's response: "Can we find the guy who can deliver the guy? We have to call the guy who calls the guy who calls the guy."

To help a client prepare for a financial transaction, we mapped backward from the target CEO to the CFO, who had earned the CEO's trust, and to an analyst who had great credibility with the CFO—and whom we had earlier prepped intensively. This made it much easier to get agreement from the CEO, who immediately turned to the CFO, who, in turn, asked the analyst, who was already on board.

Optimal sequencing decisions may defy conventional wisdom. Take, for example, the advice to "get your allies on board first." When Secretary of State James Baker was trying to build a global anti-Iraq coalition after Saddam Hussein's invasion of Kuwait, many saw Israel as America's strongest regional ally. Yet Israel was pointedly excluded: Its formal membership would have kept numerous

Sample Negotiation Campaigns

NEGOTIATION CAMPAIGNS ARE not just for huge deals. They can also be useful in a wide range of situations, whenever a series of small negotiations on various fronts is necessary to build support for a deal. Here are a few examples:

Negotiating an Industry Technology Standard

Target deal and winning coalition

You seek sustainable agreement on your company's preferred technology standard from a critical mass of key players in your industry association.

Key fronts

Supporters, competitors, undecided groups, major industry customers, regulators, trade press

Campaign approach

Your campaign must outflank backers of competing standards while generating a bandwagon of supporters, leading to a shared sense of the inevitability of your preferred standard.

Negotiating Strategic Change

Target deal and winning coalition

As a country manager of a multinational corporation in an emerging region, you seek the board's approval of a major strategic change and the support of influential corporate and regional executives in production, marketing, sales, finance, and legal functions.

Key fronts

Board of directors, senior corporate executives, functional executives at headquarters, regional country managers, regional functional managers, major customers

---

Arab states from joining. Baker and his team avoided this by treating Israel as a tacit member of the coalition (and discouraging direct Israeli retaliation against Saddam's Scud missiles).

Similarly, when preparing to negotiate on external fronts, you might be tempted to "get your own house in order first" or to start by forging an internal position. Yet in preparing for the first Gulf War, James Baker and President George H.W. Bush began by

Campaign approach

Given your lack of formal authority, start with mini-campaigns in the region and at headquarters rather than going directly to the board. During this internal campaign, you must persuade skeptical country managers, potential rivals, functional executives in the region, and key headquarters executives to support the change. You must bring these regional and corporate fronts together at the right time and in the right way to convince board members that your strategic initiative is feasible and desirable.

Negotiating Country Acceptance of a New Drug

Target deal and winning coalition

Your firm seeks approval by health authorities of a new pharmaceutical compound for specific therapeutic uses, agreement by the government to fund it, and support by key physician groups.

Key fronts

Health officials, finance officials, scientific bodies, physician groups, insurers (who may be liable for side effects of this or competing therapies), patient advocacy groups, pharmaceutical competitors, media

Campaign approach

You must orchestrate a process—partly in sequence (for fronts whose assents depend on others) and partly parallel (when fronts are largely independent)—of obtaining the agreement of key researchers on the scientific and economic merits of the drug, of generating support from physicians and patients' advocates for the new therapy, and of securing government agreement on its efficacy, political desirability, and budgetary feasibility.

committing U.S. troops to the region and then negotiated exhaustively on multiple international fronts. These efforts culminated in a UN Security Council resolution that authorized "all necessary means" to eject Iraq from Kuwait. Only after this external success did the Bush administration turn to the internal U.S. congressional front for authorization. Had Bush and Baker tried *first* to gain approval to use force from a deeply skeptical Congress, they would have almost certainly failed, which would have hobbled any subsequent American-led coalition-building enterprise. The external coalition and UN vote were crucial in getting Congress on board.

Common sequencing instincts may also lead you astray for other reasons. For example, when Steve Perlman was getting WebTV up and running, he faced multiple fronts—financial, content provider, distribution, manufacturing, and so forth—on which he could focus his small team's negotiating resources. With his venture running on financial fumes, many urged the obvious: that he focus on venture capital firms, angel investors, and industrial partners. Unfortunately for the nascent enterprise, those potential funders were deeply skeptical of consumer electronics investments. Instead of a direct approach, therefore, Perlman mapped backward from his aggressive target financial deal. He reasoned that WebTV's value would skyrocket if he could gain the support of at least one prominent consumer electronics firm. So he turned his attention to Sony and Philips, and once he had completed the difficult deals to get those giants on board, he redirected his efforts on the financial front and negotiated for much more VC money on far more advantageous terms than he could have secured earlier. With this new money, Perlman laid an intricate path of supporting agreements through the remaining fronts, including wholesale and retail distribution channels, content providers, ISPs, and alliance partners abroad. Unexpectedly, what Perlman viewed as a long-term negotiation campaign quickly reached a finale when Bill Gates expressed keen interest and Perlman negotiated the sale of his thriving young business to Microsoft.

The optimal sequence in a campaign depends on the nature of the dependencies among fronts. Focus earlier on a front when success at that stage is required for later progress or when it sends a positive signal, takes advantage of deference or influence among parties, or strengthens your later position. But early success may also come at the cost of much greater value later on, and an early failure may preclude subsequent success. (These points only scratch the surface of what is required for effective campaign-sequencing decisions.

5. Determine how much information to share and when

Your sequencing choices often determine the extent to which you reveal your activities to opponents or to various fronts. For example, you'll want it to be widely known if a savvy investor has signed on. Just as obviously, you'll want to be guarded about a failure to sign up a player known for his astute business instincts.

Public perception of the negotiation process can matter. Secrecy or hints of backroom dealings, while sometimes tactically useful, may undercut a campaign's legitimacy. For example, when the president of Honduras insisted on keeping secret an agreement on a major forestry project with Stone Container, he fueled suspicions of dirty dealings. This energized widespread opposition on several fronts—political, labor, business, environmental—and ultimately derailed an investment that promised huge economic and environmental gains for the impoverished Central American country.

For some activities, such as fundraising efforts, you'll want to be quiet until you have key pledges in hand. Revealing your interim results may then generate momentum or a sense of inevitability. In other settings, an apparent bandwagon can persuade wavering allies to join and intimidate those who might oppose you if your campaign appeared vulnerable.

In situations where information might mobilize opponents or opportunists, be discreet until you've locked in substantial progress. A classic example involves the challenge of assembling enough parcels for a major real estate development. If word leaks out about the status of individual negotiations, the risk of costly holdouts can skyrocket.

6. Learn and adapt

Campaign design and execution decisions are inherently iterative. We've listed the steps sequentially, but throughout the process new information will surface, your counterparts will react to events, and alignments and circumstances may change. You need to continually evaluate where you are and be prepared to update your strategy and tactics. The right mind-set for an effective negotiation campaigner is to think strategically but act opportunistically.

From Single Deals to Campaigns

Most negotiation scholars and popular handbooks focus on the individual deal as the unit of analysis. They probe communication patterns, tactical choices, and factors that influence the outcome of a direct approach, such as gender or culture. A negotiation campaign also calls for these analytic and behavioral skills, but only as elements of a broader, strategic approach.

When the unit of analysis shifts from one deal to a multifront campaign, the focus turns from tactics "at the table" toward a process that may unfold over months or years. Going straight to a key decision maker to negotiate often makes good sense. Yet designing and executing a negotiation campaign can sometimes be far more effective. In many cases, it's the only way.

Originally published in November 2012. Reprint R1211G

How to Make the Other Side Play Fair

by Max H. Bazerman and Daniel Kahneman

PLEASE ANSWER TWO quick questions:

1. When negotiating, do you want the other side to be reasonable?

2. Is it a good idea to be reasonable in negotiations?

Everyone we ask says yes to the first question, but answers diverge in response to the second. Academics lean toward yes, but businesspeople and lawyers often hesitate. In legal disputes, contested insurance claims, and similarly adversarial negotiations, they point out, the other party is likely to open with an inflated claim or a lowball offer. If the other side's position is unreasonable, these practitioners suggest, it makes little sense to be reasonable yourself.

Suppose a customer claims that a problem with a product you sold him resulted in a $10 million loss to his business. After careful analysis, your legal team concludes that the fair value of his claim is just $5 million. How do you respond? A common reflex is to come back with, say, $1 million. The familiar and dysfunctional negotiation dance that follows can be costly for all involved. The parties may eventually converge on a figure close to $5 million, but only after spending a lot of time and money to get there—and harming their relationship in the process.

It would be to everyone's advantage if parties routinely came to a negotiation with a reasonable offer in hand: If starting positions are realistic, the offers will be more or less aligned, and any negotiation that follows should be relatively civil, speedy, and fair. But how can a negotiator who wants to be fair from the start ensure that his or her counterpart will be reasonable as well?

This question inspired us to propose the *final-offer arbitration challenge,* a new negotiation strategy for reaching fair agreements efficiently, even when dealing with seemingly unreasonable opponents. Leveraging an approach first applied in labor negotiations in the 1960s, the strategy allows one side to encourage reasonableness on the part of the other by making a demonstrably fair offer at the outset and then, if the other side is unreasonable, challenging it to take the competing offers to an arbitrator who must choose one or the other rather than a compromise between them. We conceived the final-offer arbitration challenge in the course of our work with the global insurance company AIG. As we'll describe, the strategy could be used in negotiations well beyond insurance.

The Challenge in Action

Insurance companies pay billions of dollars every year to settle claims, employing hundreds of people to evaluate and negotiate tens of thousands of cases. There is good reason to believe that their employees' decisions are not always optimal, resulting in overpayment on some claims and needlessly costly negotiation over others. AIG's CEO, Peter Hancock, who was familiar with Daniel Kahneman's *Thinking, Fast and Slow,* invited TGG, the consulting firm with which Kahneman is affiliated, to explore solutions. Kahneman recruited Max Bazerman to examine the company's approach to negotiation. What began as a brief engagement became a large-scale, long-term project to sharpen AIG's ability to efficiently resolve claims and reach reasonable settlements, reduce costs, and improve its reputation for fairness. Success with this intervention, Hancock reasoned, could ultimately confer competitive advantage.

AIG used the final-offer arbitration challenge in a difficult negotiation with a man who had been injured while working in a factory it insured. The company didn't want to overpay on the claim, but it also didn't want to appear unfair in the eyes of its

Idea in Brief

The Problem

The two sides in an adversarial negotiation rarely bring their most reasonable offers to the table. Rather, each stakes out a position to its advantage and seeks to give up as little as possible. This common approach is often costly to all involved.

The Solution

A new negotiation strategy can efficiently lead to an equitable agreement: One side presents an objectively fair offer, challenging the other to make its own best offer and then allow an arbitrator to decide which of the two is more reasonable.

The Result

The threat of losing in a final-offer arbitration will typically bring an unreasonable adversary back to the table with a more reasonable offer. The insurance giant AIG tested this strategy in an injury claims case, leading to a rapid, fair settlement.

customer, the factory owner. Drawing on the assessments of several outside experts, AIG estimated the claim's fair value at $1 million to $1.1 million and made an offer of $850,000. The claimant's attorney countered with $2.6 million—an amount he vehemently insisted was fair.

AIG, confident that its position was reasonable (and that the claimant's wasn't), responded with a final-offer arbitration challenge: Present the two offers to a professional arbitrator, who would make a legally binding decision about which was more reasonable. By forbidding an arbitrator to split the difference between two offers, this procedure neutralizes any incentive to be unreasonable, because the arbitrator is unlikely to choose the less reasonable offer. (See the sidebar "A Primer on Final-Offer Arbitration.") In a conventional arbitration or a typical judicial process, the arbitrator *is* allowed to choose a value between the two figures. Although conventional arbitration may be efficient in comparison with a lengthy court process, it tends to reward unreasonableness, because the parties believe that the arbitrator will land somewhere between their offers. The more unreasonable your offer is, therefore, the better you are likely to fare.

A Primer on Final-Offer Arbitration

FINAL-OFFER ARBITRATION—also known as "baseball arbitration" because of its use in Major League Baseball salary disputes—was first suggested in the 1960s by the labor relations scholar Carl Stevens as a strategy for driving parties to agreement. Conventional arbitration was already in frequent use as an alternative to strikes for resolving disagreements between management and labor. In conventional arbitration the two parties make their cases to a neutral third party whose ruling on the issue at stake is binding.

Essentially, conventional arbitration serves as an efficient judicial process. But research showed that parties were remaining far apart in the expectation that the arbitrator would simply split the difference between them. In that case, the more unreasonable your offer, the better you fared. Thus many people questioned the wisdom of arbitration. Stevens created final-offer arbitration to address the problem and to encourage negotiators to solve disputes on their own.

Under final-offer arbitration, reasonableness is rewarded rather than punished. The two parties submit their final offers, and the arbitrator must select one or the other. Although this may prevent the arbitrator from choosing a number he or she believes is truly fair, the riskiness of the process drives the parties toward agreement, dramatically raising settlement rates. In the rare case when arbitration is actually invoked, each party competes to be more reasonable than the other.

"The suggestion was not received with overwhelming enthusiasm by the labor-relations community," Stevens recounted in 1976. "Indeed, there was a tendency to write it off as an unworkable 'gimmick.'" Many people criticized the requirement that the arbitrator choose the lesser of two evils rather than what was actually fair. Nevertheless, final-offer arbitration has proved to be a strong alternative to courts and strikes.

The final-offer arbitration challenge worked because it exposed the unreasonableness of the other side's position: The claimant's attorney, realizing that AIG was convinced of its position and unlikely to be flexible, abruptly reduced the demand by more than half, from $2.6 million to $1.25 million. AIG reiterated its relatively fair offer of $850,000. A rapid series of offers and counteroffers ensued, and the claim was settled in a matter of days for $1.05 million.

Notice that the parties in this case ultimately avoided arbitration but did converge on a number close to AIG's opening offer. We expect that as the challenge strategy is used more widely, this result will be common: The party subject to the challenge will quickly return to the table with a more reasonable position.

It is rational for claims executives to argue that if they make a reasonable opening offer of 90% of a claim's true value and the other side counters with an unreasonable 1,000%, they will be poorly positioned for the usual process of exchanging concessions. The final-offer arbitration challenge curtails this process by sending a credible signal that the other side should not expect much more movement. We are confident that the challenge will often bring the other party to reasonableness.

When to Use the Challenge

Prior to this work, the use of arbitration was typically established as the default for obtaining agreement long before the actual negotiation started. That is, it was mandated if the parties couldn't reach an agreement on their own. A unique feature of our approach is that one side in a dispute can present the final-offer arbitration challenge at any time.

We suggest that parties we are advising determine, before or during a negotiation, the range of possible settlements an objective observer would consider fair and then make a reasonable offer. If the counteroffer is unreasonable, they should ask if the other side really believes that its offer is fair. If the answer is yes, they should propose that the two offers be submitted to final-offer arbitration. If you are sure that your offer is more reasonable than the counteroffer, you can be confident of prevailing if the other side accepts the challenge. But it rarely will. The point of the challenge is to credibly signal that you believe your offer is fair and you won't improve on it unless the other side returns to the table with a far more reasonable proposal.

The challenge strategy makes sense in any dispute where four conditions are met: You have made a reasonable offer that has been countered with an unreasonable one. You are confident of what a fair resolution would be. Escalating the dispute into litigation would be costly. Neither side can easily walk away.

What is "fair" or "reasonable" lies on a spectrum from objective to subjective and thus from clear to ambiguous. With many insurance or legal claims, historical data or records from similar cases can provide a solid basis for determining a fair settlement. The value of a new car totaled in an accident is easy to determine and hard to dispute. But personal injury claims involving emotional suffering require more-subjective evaluations. The challenge should be reserved for disputes in which the objective value of a claim is fairly clear; the more ambiguous the value, the greater the uncertainty about where an arbitrator's decision will fall.

To determine fairness in an injury case, an insurance company could assemble several independent experts, give them the facts, and ask each to gauge the claim's value. If their conclusions are fairly well aligned, the insurer can be confident of its offer. If a group of experts returns with widely divergent values, you know that "fair" is ambiguous—and, therefore, that using the challenge strategy will be risky.

Having established what's fair, ask, "Can either party easily walk away?" In a typical buyer-seller transaction, if the parties' positions are polarized and neither side is inclined to bargain, a final-offer arbitration challenge isn't useful, because the other side can simply abandon the negotiation. In a legal dispute, however, where walking away isn't an option, the strategy can make sense.

This approach is most applicable to resolving disputes, but we can also imagine how it might help close a deal. For example, it could be used to break an impasse in a merger negotiation when the parties have agreed to all but one of the deal's components. Rather than allow the negotiation to collapse over one small dispute, the parties could subject the lone contested element to final-offer arbitration, potentially preserving the merger. (See the sidebar "Saving the Deal.")

Building Your Reputation

The obvious benefit of employing this strategy is economic: A more efficient negotiation is a lower-cost negotiation. But the strategy potentially has another, less obvious benefit—enhancing a company's reputation for fairness. That was one of Peter Hancock's goals. Several considerations are relevant when using the strategy to this end.

We recommend that you begin a negotiation with a reasonable offer—to the extent that you have a good assessment of what is fair—and that you do so before an unreasonable one is put on the table. This flies in the face of much conventional wisdom, but it will strengthen the reputational signal you're trying to send. (It will also leverage the anchoring effect, steering the other side toward reasonableness from the start.) In a more typical negotiation, both parties open with unreasonable positions and only later move to a reasonable stance. But if the goal is to signal fairness, beginning the dysfunctional dance will work against you.

We discourage use of the challenge when both sides are being unreasonable. Although you may win the dispute, you won't have improved your reputation—and you may have diminished it. Furthermore, it's highly uncertain what an arbitrator faced with two unreasonable offers will decide.

Getting Started

Companies interested in using the final-offer arbitration challenge will most likely pilot it. If that goes well, they may choose to roll it out more widely. Adding the challenge strategy to a tool kit requires developing new negotiation skills and may mean leading a significant organizational culture change. As noted, opening a negotiation with their most reasonable position is anathema to many practitioners.

Let's look first at the technical part—learning new skills. In most companies where some negotiation ability is required, basic soft skills—such as how to read the other side or find opportunities for joint gain—are commonly taught. But companies rarely teach the negotiation analytics skills that business schools do. A company planning to use our strategy must train its negotiators to objectively assess fairness—including how to conduct formal analysis on the basis of previous negotiations and how to aggregate assessments

Saving the Deal

CONSIDER HOW the final-offer arbitration challenge might be used to rescue a merger negotiation when the parties are close to an acquisition price. The target firm wishes to reach agreement quickly to avoid a hostile takeover attempt by a different company. The target and the acquirer are only $30 million apart—a small percentage of the roughly $800 million price. The disagreement is over the valuation of one piece of the business: a new project about which the target, unlike the acquirer, is enthusiastic. There is not enough time to extract this project from the deal—for example, by selling it off as a separate company.

Either side could propose moving forward with the agreement while quickly setting up final-offer arbitration to determine whose valuation of the project is fairer. We predict that such a proposal would result in a negotiated agreement, making the arbitration unnecessary. And if either side was bluffing about its valuation of the new project, the final-offer arbitration challenge should bring it back to the table in a more concessionary mood.

---

from multiple experts. And, of course, negotiators must learn the mechanics of issuing the final-offer arbitration challenge. They need to be instructed in the legal logistics of setting up the process, local arbitration laws in countries around the world, and how to access arbitrators through organizations such as the American Arbitration Association.

These methods have been disseminated across AIG through an international training program we devised for many hundreds of adjusters involved in claims worth tens of billions of dollars. An important part of the training has been to teach skeptical adjusters the logic of abandoning negotiation tactics they've long found natural. Getting buy-in for the new approach, which puts being fair first, is essential.

The leadership challenge can't be overemphasized. Although leaders at the highest level may see an argument for change, those further down in the managerial ranks may push back against doing some things very differently. Actively creating a supportive environment means rewarding negotiators for using the strategy—and not punishing them for negative outcomes.

Suppose a claims adjuster proposes final-offer arbitration and his company loses. That's not necessarily a bad thing; the company shouldn't expect to win every case that goes to arbitration. Consistent success might suggest that the company tends to make overly generous offers. However, if the gap between the competing offers was large and the company's negotiator lost, he or she may have misjudged what constituted a reasonable offer. To reduce the danger of such misjudgments, we propose that a broader team, including the negotiator's manager, review the offer in advance. When a bad outcome suggests a misjudgment, the company—not an individual negotiator—should own the decision.

Above all, it's critical that endorsement of the program at the highest level be visible throughout the organization. At AIG materials for the training program were conspicuously branded "The AIG Way of Negotiating," and Hancock publicly emphasized both the reduced litigation costs and the reputational benefits he hoped would result.

We encourage negotiators to use the final-offer arbitration challenge not as a hostile act but as a civil mechanism for signaling an honest belief in the fairness of their offers. Fully implementing the strategy requires leadership commitment and investments in training. But if it reduces costs, improves customer satisfaction, and boosts your reputation, the investment is sure to be worthwhile.

Originally published in September 2016. Reprint R1609F

Getting Past Yes

Negotiating as if implementation mattered. *by Danny Ertel*

IN JULY 1998, AT&T and BT announced a new 50/50 joint venture that promised to bring global interconnectivity to multinational customers. Concert, as the venture was called, was launched with great fanfare and even greater expectations: The $10 billion start-up would pool assets, talent, and relationships and was expected to log $1 billion in profits from day one. Just three years later, Concert was out of business. It had laid off 2,300 employees, announced $7 billion in charges, and returned its infrastructure assets to the parent companies. To be sure, the weak market played a role in Concert's demise, but the way the deal was put together certainly hammered a few nails into the coffin.

For example, AT&T's deal makers scored what they probably considered a valuable win when they negotiated a way for AT&T Solutions to retain key multinational customers for itself. As a result, AT&T and BT ended up in direct competition for business—exactly what the Concert venture was supposed to help prevent. For its part, BT seemingly outnegotiated AT&T by refusing to contribute to AT&T's purchase of the IBM Global Network. That move saved BT money, but it muddied Concert's strategy, leaving the start-up to contend with overlapping products. In 2000, Concert announced a complex new arrangement that was supposed to clarify its strategy, but many questions about account ownership, revenue recognition, and competing offerings went unanswered. Ultimately, the two parent companies pulled the plug on the venture.[1]

Concert is hardly the only alliance that began with a signed contract and a champagne toast but ended in bitter disappointment. Examples abound of deals that look terrific on paper but never materialize into effective, value-creating endeavors. And it's not just alliances that can go bad during implementation. Misfortune can befall a whole range of agreements that involve two or more parties—mergers, acquisitions, outsourcing contracts, even internal projects that require the cooperation of more than one department. Although the problem often masquerades as one of execution, its roots are anchored in the deal's inception, when negotiators act as if their main objective were to sign the deal. To be successful, negotiators must recognize that signing a contract is just the beginning of the process of creating value.

During the past 20 years, I've analyzed or assisted in hundreds of complex negotiations, both through my research at the Harvard Negotiation Project and through my consulting practice. And I've seen countless deals that were signed with optimism fall apart during implementation, despite the care and creativity with which their terms were crafted. The crux of the problem is that the very person everyone thinks is central to the deal—the negotiator—is often the one who undermines the partnership's ability to succeed. The real challenge lies not in hammering out little victories on the way to signing on the dotted line but in designing a deal that works in practice.

The Danger of Deal Makers

It's easy to see where the deal maker mind-set comes from. The media glorifies big-name deal makers like Donald Trump, Michael Ovitz, and Bruce Wasserstein. Books like *You Can Negotiate Anything, Trump: The Art of the Deal*, and even my own partners' *Getting to Yes*, all position the end of the negotiation as the destination. And most companies evaluate and compensate negotiators based on the size of the deals they're signing.

Idea in Brief

Why do so many deals that looked great on paper end up in tatters? Negotiators on both sides probably focused too much on closing the deals and squeezing the best terms out of one another—and not enough on implementation. Bargainers with this **deal maker mind-set** never ask how—or whether—their agreement will work *in practice*. Once implementation begins, surprises and disappointments crop up—often torpedoing the deal.

How to avoid this scenario? Bargain using an **implementation mind-set**. Define negotiation not as closing the deal but as setting the stage for a successful long-term relationship. Brainstorm and discuss problems you might encounter 12 months down the road. Help the other party think through the agreement's practical implications, so your counterparts won't promise something they can't deliver. Ensure that both sides' stakeholders support the deal. And communicate a consistent message about the deal's terms and spirit to both parties' implementation teams.

Deals negotiated from an implementation mind-set don't "sizzle" like those struck by bargainers practicing brinksmanship. But as companies like HP Services and Procter & Gamble have discovered, a deal's real value comes not from a signature on a document but from the real work performed long after the ink has dried.

But what kind of behavior does this approach create? People who view the contract as the conclusion and see themselves as solely responsible for getting there behave very differently from those who see the agreement as just the beginning and believe their role is to ensure that the parties involved actually realize the value they are trying to create. These two camps have conflicting opinions about the use of surprise and the sharing of information. They also differ in how much attention they pay to whether the parties' commitments are realistic, whether their stakeholders are sufficiently aligned, and whether those who must implement the deal can establish a suitable working relationship with one another. (For a comparison of how different mind-sets affect negotiation behaviors, see the exhibit "Deal-minded negotiators versus implementation-minded negotiators.")

Idea in Practice

To adopt an implementation mind-set, apply these practices *before* inking a deal:

Start with the End in Mind

Imagine that it's a year into implementation of your deal. Ask:

- **Is the deal working?** What metrics are you using to measure its success?

- **What has gone wrong so far?** What have you done to put things back on course? What signals suggest trouble ahead?

- **What capabilities are needed to accomplish the deal's objectives?** What skills do your implementation teams need? Who has tried to block implementation, and how have you responded?

By answering these questions now, you avoid being blindsided by surprises during implementation.

Help the Other Party Prepare

Coming to the table prepared to negotiate a workable deal isn't enough—your *counterpart* must also prepare. Before negotiations begin, encourage the other party to consult with their internal stakeholders throughout the bargaining process. Explain who you think the key players are, who should be involved early on, and what key questions about implementation you're asking yourself.

Treat Alignment as a Shared Responsibility

Jointly address how you'll build broad support for the deal's

This isn't to say deal makers are sleazy, dishonest, or unethical. Being a deal maker means being a good closer. The deal maker mind-set is the ideal approach in certain circumstances. For example, when negotiating the sale of an asset in which title will simply be transferred and the parties will have little or no need to work together, getting the signatures on the page really does define success.

But frequently a signed contract represents a commitment to work together to create value. When that's the case, the manner in which the parties "get to yes" matters a great deal. Unfortunately, many organizations structure their negotiation teams and manage the flow of information in ways that actually hurt a deal's chances of being implemented well.

An organization that embraces the deal maker approach, for instance, tends to structure its business development teams in a

implementation. Identify both parties' stakeholders—those who will make decisions, affect the deal's success through action or inaction, hold critical budgets, or possess crucial information. Map how and when different stakeholders' input will be solicited. Ask who needs to know what in order to support the deal and carry out their part of its implementation.

Send One Message

Ensure that each team responsible for implementing the deal understands what the agreement is meant to accomplish. Communicate *one* message to them about the terms of the deal, the spirit in which it was negotiated, and the trade-offs that were made to craft the final contract.

Example: During IBM Global Services' "joint handoff meetings," the company's negotiators *and* their counterparts brief implementation teams on what's in the contract, what's different or nonstandard, and what the deal's ultimate intent is.

Manage Negotiation Like a Business Process

Establish a disciplined process for negotiation preparation in your company. Provide training in collaborative negotiation tools and techniques for negotiators *and* implementers. Use post-negotiation reviews to capture learning. And reward individuals for the delivered success of the deals they negotiated—not for how those deals look on paper.

---

way that drives an ever growing stream of new deals. These dedicated teams, responsible for keeping negotiations on track and getting deals done, build tactical expertise, acquire knowledge of useful contract terms, and go on to sign more deals. But they also become detached from implementation and are likely to focus more on the agreement than on its business impact. Just think about the language deal-making teams use ("closing" a deal, putting a deal "to bed") and how their performance is measured and rewarded (in terms of the number and size of deals closed and the time required to close them). These teams want to sign a piece of paper and book the expected value; they couldn't care less about launching a relationship.

The much-talked-about Business Affairs engine at AOL under David Colburn is one extreme example. The group became so

Deal-minded negotiators versus implementation-minded negotiators

Deal-minded negotiators	Negotiation tactics	Implementation-minded negotiators
Assumption "Surprising them helps me. They may commit to something they might not have otherwise, and we'll get a better deal." **Behaviors** • Introduce new actors or information at strategic points in the negotiation. • Raise new issues at the end.	= *Surprise* =	**Assumption** "Surprising them puts us at risk. They may commit to something they cannot deliver or will regret." **Behaviors** • Propose agendas in advance so both parties can prepare. • Suggest questions to be discussed, and provide relevant data. • Raise issues early.
Assumption "It's not my role to equip them with relevant information or to correct their misperceptions." **Behaviors** • Withhold information. • Fail to correct mistaken impressions.	= *Information sharing* =	**Assumption** "I don't want them entering this deal feeling duped. I want their goodwill during implementation, not their grudging compliance." **Behaviors** • Create a joint fact-gathering group. • Commission third-party research and analysis. • Question everyone's assumptions openly.
Assumption "My job is to get the deal closed. It's worth putting a little pressure on them now and coping with their unhappiness later." **Behaviors** • Create artificial deadlines. • Threaten escalation. • Make "this day only" offers.	= *Closing techniques* =	**Assumption** "My job is to create value by crafting a workable agreement. Investing a little extra time in making sure both sides are aligned is worth the effort." **Behaviors** • Define interests that need to be considered for the deal to be successful. • Define joint communication strategy.

Assumption

"As long as they commit, that's all that matters. Afterward, it's their problem if they don't deliver."

Behaviors

- Focus on documenting commitments rather than on testing the practicality of those commitments.
- Rely on penalty clauses for protection.

= *Realistic commitments* =

Assumption

"If they fail to deliver, we don't get the value we expect."

Behaviors

- Ask tough questions about both parties' ability to deliver.
- Make implementability a shared concern.
- Establish early warning systems and contingency plans.

Assumption

"The fewer people involved in making this decision, the better and faster this will go."

Behaviors

- Limit participation in discussions to decision makers.
- Keep outsiders in the dark until it is too late for them to derail things.

= *Decision making and stakeholders* =

Assumption

"If we both fail to involve key stakeholders sufficiently and early enough, whatever time we save now will be lost during implementation."

Behaviors

- Repeatedly ask about stakeholders:
- Whose approval is needed?
- Whose cooperation is required?
- Who might interfere with implementation?

focused on doing deals—the larger and more lopsided the better—that it lost sight of the need to have its business partners actually remain in business or to have its deals produce more than paper value. In 2002, following internal investigations and probes by the SEC and the Department of Justice, AOL Time Warner concluded it needed to restate financial results to account for the real value (or lack thereof) created by some of those deals.[2]

The deal maker mentality also fosters the take-no-prisoners attitude common in procurement organizations. The aim: Squeeze your counterpart for the best possible deal you can get. Instead of focusing on deal volume, as business development engines do, these groups concentrate on how many concessions they can get. The desire to win outweighs the costs of signing a deal that cannot work in practice because the supplier will never be able to make enough money.

Think about how companies handle negotiations with outsourcing providers. Few organizations contract out enough of their work to have as much expertise as the providers themselves in negotiating deal structures, terms and conditions, metrics, pricing, and the like, so they frequently engage a third-party adviser to help level the playing field as they select an outsourcer and hammer out a contract. Some advisers actually trumpet their role in commoditizing the providers' solutions so they can create "apples to apples" comparison charts, engender competitive bidding, and drive down prices. To maximize competitive tension, they exert tight control, blocking virtually all communications between would-be customers and service providers. That means the outsourcers have almost no opportunity to design solutions tailored to the customer's unique business drivers.

The results are fairly predictable. The deal structure that both customer and provider teams are left to implement is the one that was easiest to compare with other bids, not the one that would have created the most value. Worse yet, when the negotiators on each side exit the process, the people responsible for making the deal work are virtual strangers and lack a nuanced understanding of why issues were handled the way they were. Furthermore, neither side has earned the trust of its partner during negotiations. The hard feelings created by the hired guns can linger for years.

The fact is, organizations that depend on negotiations for growth can't afford to abdicate management responsibility for the process. It would be foolhardy to leave negotiations entirely up to the individual wits and skills of those sitting at the table on any given day. That's why some corporations have taken steps to make negotiation an organizational competence. They have made the process more structured by, for instance, applying Six Sigma discipline or community of practice principles to improve outcomes and learn from past experiences.

Sarbanes-Oxley and an emphasis on greater management accountability will only reinforce this trend. As more companies (and their auditors) recognize the need to move to a controls-based approach for their deal-making processes—be they in sales, sourcing, or business development—they will need to implement metrics, tools, and process disciplines that preserve creativity and let managers truly manage negotiators. How they do so, and how they define the role of the negotiator, will determine whether deals end up creating or destroying value.

Negotiating for Implementation

Making the leap to an implementation mind-set requires five shifts.

1. Start with the end in mind

For the involved parties to reap the benefits outlined in the agreement, goodwill and collaboration are needed during implementation. That's why negotiation teams should carry out a simple "benefit of hindsight" exercise as part of their preparation.

Imagine that it is 12 months into the deal, and ask yourself:

Is the deal working? What metrics are we using? If quantitative metrics are too hard to define, what other indications of success can we use?

A New Mind-Set

FIVE APPROACHES can help your negotiating team transition from a deal maker mentality to an implementation mind-set.

1. **Start with the end in mind.** Imagine the deal 12 months out: What has gone wrong? How do you know if it's a success? Who should have been involved earlier?

2. **Help them prepare, too.** Surprising the other side doesn't make sense, because if they promise things they can't deliver, you both lose.

3. **Treat alignment as a shared responsibility.** If your counterpart's interests aren't aligned, it's your problem, too.

4. **Send one message.** Brief implementation teams on both sides of the deal together so everyone has the same information.

5. **Manage negotiation like a business process.** Combine a disciplined preparation process with postnegotiation reviews.

What has gone wrong so far? What have we done to put things back on course? What were some early warning signals that the deal may not meet its objectives?

What capabilities are necessary to accomplish our objectives? What processes and tools must be in place? What skills must the implementation teams have? What attitudes or assumptions are required of those who must implement the deal? Who has tried to block implementation, and how have we responded?

If negotiators are required to answer those kinds of questions before the deal is finalized, they cannot help but behave differently. For example, if the negotiators of the Concert joint venture had followed that line of questioning before closing the deal, they might have asked themselves, "What good is winning the right to keep customers out of the deal if doing so leads to competition between the alliance's parents? And if we have to take that risk, can we put in mechanisms now to help mitigate it?" Raising those tough questions probably wouldn't have made a negotiator popular, but it might have led to different terms in the deal and certainly to different processes and metrics in the implementation plan.

Most organizations with experience in negotiating complex deals know that some terms have a tendency to come back and bite them during implementation. For example, in 50/50 ventures, the partner with greater leverage often secures the right to break ties if the new venture's steering committee should ever come to an impasse on an issue. In practice, though, that means executives from the dominant party who go into negotiations to resolve such impasses don't really have to engage with the other side. At the end of the day, they know they can simply impose their decision. But when that happens, the relationship is frequently broken beyond repair.

Tom Finn, vice president of strategic planning and alliances at Procter & Gamble Pharmaceuticals, has made it his mission to incorporate tough lessons like that into the negotiation process itself. Although Finn's alliance management responsibilities technically don't start until after a deal has been negotiated by the P&G Pharmaceuticals business development organization, Finn jumps into the negotiation process to ensure negotiators do not bargain for terms that will cause trouble down the road. "It's not just a matter of a win-win philosophy," he says. "It's about incorporating our alliance managers' hard-won experience with terms that cause implementation problems and not letting those terms into our deals."

Finn and his team avoid things like step-down royalties and unequal profit splits with 50/50 expense sharing, to name just a few. "It's important that the partners be provided [with] incentives to do the right thing," Finn says. "When those incentives shift, you tend to end up [with] difficulties." Step-down royalties, for instance, are a common structure in the industry. They're predicated on the assumption that a brand is made or lost in the first three years so that thereafter, payments to the originator should go down. But P&G Pharmaceuticals believes it is important to provide incentives to the partner to continue to work hard over time. As for concerns about overpaying for the licensed compound in the latter years of the contract, Finn asserts that "leaving some money on the table is OK if you realize that the most expensive deal is one that fails."

2. Help them prepare, too

If implementation is the name of the game, then coming to the table well prepared is necessary—but not sufficient. Your counterpart must also be prepared to negotiate a workable deal. Some negotiators believe they can gain advantage by surprising the other side. But surprise confers advantage only because the counterpart has failed to think through all the implications of a proposal and might mistakenly commit to something it wouldn't have if it had been better prepared. While that kind of an advantage might pay off in a simple buy-sell transaction, it fails miserably—for both sides—in any situation that requires a long-term working relationship.

That's why it's in your best interest to engage with your counterpart before negotiations start. Encourage the other party to do its homework and consult with its internal stakeholders before and throughout the negotiation process. Let the team know who you think the key players are, who should be involved early on, how you hope to build implementation planning into the negotiation process, and what key questions you are asking yourself.

Take the example of Equitas, a major reinsurer in the London market. When preparing for commutations negotiations—whereby two reinsurers settle their mutual book of business—the company sends its counterpart a thorough kickoff package, which is used as the agenda for the negotiation launch meeting. This "commutations action pack" describes how the reinsurer's own commutations department is organized, what its preferred approach to a commutations negotiation is, and what stages it follows. It also includes a suggested approach to policy reconciliation and due diligence and explains what data the reinsurer has available—even acknowledging its imperfections and gaps. The package describes critical issues for the reinsurer and provides sample agreements and memorandums for various stages of the process.

The kickoff meeting thus offers a structured environment in which the parties can educate each other on their decision-making processes and their expectations for the deal. The language of the commutations action pack and the collaborative spirit of the kickoff meeting are designed to help the parties get to know each other and settle on a way of working together before they start making the difficult trade-offs that will be required of them. By establishing an agreed-upon process for how and when to communicate with brokers about the deal, the two sides are better able to manage the tension between the need to include stakeholders who are critical to implementation and the need to maintain confidentiality before the deal is signed.

Aventis Pharma is another example of how measured disclosure of background and other information can pave the way to smoother negotiations and stronger implementation. Like many of its peers, the British pharmaceutical giant wants potential biotech partners to see it as a partner of choice and value a relationship with the company for more than the size of the royalty check involved. To that end, Aventis has developed and piloted a "negotiation launch" process, which it describes as a meeting during which parties about to enter into formal negotiations plan together for those negotiations. Such collaboration allows both sides to identify potential issues and set up an agreed-upon process and time line. The company asserts that while "formally launching negotiations with a counterpart may seem unorthodox to some," the entire negotiation process runs more efficiently and effectively when partners "take the time to discuss how they will negotiate before beginning."

3. Treat alignment as a shared responsibility
If their interests are not aligned, and they cannot deliver fully, that's not just their problem—it's your problem, too.

Unfortunately, deal makers often rely on secrecy to achieve their goals (after all, a stakeholder who doesn't know about a deal can't object). But leaving internal stakeholders in the dark about a potential deal can have negative consequences. Individuals and departments that will be directly affected don't have a chance to weigh in with suggestions to mitigate risks or improve the outcome. And people with relevant information about the deal don't share it, because they have no idea it's needed. Instead, the typical reaction managers have when confronted late in the game with news of a deal that will affect their department is "Not with my FTEs, you don't."

Turning a blind eye to likely alignment problems on the other side of the table is one of the leading reasons alliances break down and one of the major sources of conflict in outsourcing deals. Many companies, for instance, have outsourced some of their human resource or finance and accounting processes. Service providers, for their part, often move labor-intensive processes to web-based self-service systems to gain process efficiencies. If users find the new self-service system frustrating or intimidating, though, they make repeated (and expensive) calls to service centers or fax in handwritten forms. As a result, processing costs jump from pennies per transaction to tens of dollars per transaction.

But during the initial negotiation, buyers routinely fail to disclose just how undisciplined their processes are and how resistant to change their cultures might be. After all, they think, those problems will be the provider's headache once the deal is signed. Meanwhile, to make requested price concessions, providers often drop line items from their proposals intended to educate employees and support the new process. In exchange for such concessions, with a wink and a nod, negotiators assure the provider that the buyers will dedicate internal resources to change-management and communication efforts. No one asks whether business unit managers support the deal or whether function leaders are prepared to make the transition from managing the actual work to managing the relationship with an external provider. Everyone simply agrees, the deal is signed, and the frustration begins.

As managers and employees work around the new self-service system, the provider's costs increase, the service levels fall (because the provider was not staffed for the high level of calls and faxes), and customer satisfaction plummets. Finger-pointing ensues, which must then be addressed through expensive additions to the contract, costly modifications to processes and technology, and additional burdens on a communication and change effort already laden with baggage from the initial failure.

Building alignment is among negotiators' least favorite activities. The deal makers often feel as if they are wasting precious time "negotiating internally" instead of working their magic on the other side. But without acceptance of the deal by those who are essential to its implementation (or who can place obstacles in the way), proceeding with the deal is even more wasteful. Alignment is a classic "pay me now or pay me later" problem. To understand whether the deal will work in practice, the negotiation process must encompass not only subject matter experts or those with bargaining authority but also those who will actually have to take critical actions or refrain from pursuing conflicting avenues later.

Because significant deals often require both parties to preserve some degree of confidentiality, the matter of involving the right stakeholders at the right time is more effectively addressed jointly than unilaterally. With an understanding of who the different stakeholders are—including those who have necessary information, those who hold critical budgets, those who manage important third-party relationships, and so on—a joint communications subteam can then map how, when, and with whom different inputs will be solicited and different categories of information might be shared. For example, some stakeholders may need to know that the negotiations are taking place but not the identity of the counterpart. Others may need only to be aware that the organization is seeking to form a partnership so they can prepare for the potential effects of an eventual deal. And while some must remain in the dark, suitable proxies should be identified to ensure that their perspectives (and the roles they will play during implementation) are considered at the table.

4. Send one message
Complex deals require the participation of many people during implementation, so once the agreement is in place, it's essential that the team that created it get everyone up to speed on the terms of the deal, on the mind-set under which it was negotiated, and on the trade-offs that were made in crafting the final contract. When each implementation team is given the contract in a vacuum and then is left to interpret it separately, each develops a different picture of what the deal is meant to accomplish, of the negotiators' intentions, and of what wasn't actually written in the document but each had imagined would be true in practice.

"If your objective is to have a deal you can implement, then you want the actual people who will be there, after the negotiators move on, up front and listening to the dialogue and the give-and-take during the negotiation so they understand how you got to the agreed solution," says Steve Fenn, vice president for retail industry and former VP for global business development at IBM Global Services. "But we can't always have the delivery executive at the table, and our customer doesn't always know who from their side is going to be around to lead the relationship." To address this challenge, Fenn uses joint hand-off meetings, at which he and his counterpart brief both sides of the delivery equation. "We tell them what's in the contract, what is different or nonstandard, what the schedules cover. But more important, we clarify the intent of the deal: Here's what we had difficulty with, and here's what we ended up with and why. We don't try to reinterpret the language of the contract, but [we do try] to discuss openly the spirit of the contract." These meetings are usually attended by the individual who developed the statement of work, the person who priced the deal, the contracts and negotiation lead, and occasionally legal counsel. This team briefs the project executive in charge of the implementation effort and the executive's direct reports. Participation on the customer side varies, because the early days in an outsourcing relationship are often hectic and full of turnover. But Fenn works with the project executive and the sales team to identify the key customer representatives who should be invited to the hand-off briefing.

Negotiators who know they have to brief the implementation team with their counterparts after the deal is signed will approach the entire negotiation differently. They'll start asking the sort of tough questions at the negotiating table that they imagine they'll have to field during the postdeal briefings. And as they think about how they will explain the deal to the delivery team, they will begin to marshal defensible precedents, norms, industry practices, and objective criteria. Such standards of legitimacy strengthen the relationship because they emphasize persuasion rather than coercion. Ultimately, this practice makes a deal more viable because attention shifts from the individual negotiators and their personalities toward the merits of the arrangement.

5. Manage negotiation like a business process

Negotiating as if implementation mattered isn't a simple task. You must worry about the costs and challenges of execution rather than just getting the other side to say yes. You must carry out all the internal consultations necessary to build alignment. And you must make sure your counterparts are as prepared as you are. Each of these actions can feel like a big time sink. Deal makers don't want to spend time negotiating with their own people to build alignment or risk having their counterparts pull out once they know all the details. If a company wants its negotiators to sign deals that create real value, though, it has to weed out that deal maker mentality from its ranks. Fortunately, it can be done with simple processes and controls. (For an example of how HP Services structures its negotiation process, see the sidebar "Negotiating Credibility.")

More and more outsourcing and procurement firms are adopting a disciplined negotiation preparation process. Some even require a manager to review the output of that process before authorizing the negotiator to proceed with the deal. KLA-Tencor, a semiconductor production equipment maker, uses the electronic tools available through its supplier-management website for this purpose, for example. Its managers can capture valuable information about negotiators' practices, including the issues they are coming up against, the options they are proposing, the standards of legitimacy they are relying on, and the walkaway alternatives they are considering. Coupled with simple postnegotiation reviews, this information can yield powerful organizational insights.

Preparing for successful implementation is hard work, and it has a lot less sizzle than the brinksmanship characteristic of the negotiation process itself. To overcome the natural tendency to ignore feasibility questions, it's important for management to send a clear message about the value of postdeal implementation. It must reward individuals, at least in part, based on the delivered success of the deals they negotiate, not on how those deals look on paper. This practice is fairly standard among outsourcing service providers; it's one that should be adopted more broadly.

Negotiating Credibility

HP SERVICES is growing in a highly competitive market, and its success is partly due to its approach to negotiating large outsourcing transactions. In a maturing market, where top-tier providers can demonstrate comparable capabilities and where price variations inevitably diminish after companies bid against one another time and time again, a provider's ability to manage a relationship and build trust are key differentiators. The negotiation and the set of interactions leading up to it give the customer a first taste of what it will be like to solve problems with the provider during the life of the contract. "Decisions made by clients regarding selection have as much to do with the company they want to do business with as with price, capability, and reliability," acknowledges Steve Huhn, HP Services' vice president of strategic outsourcing. "Negotiating these kinds of deals requires being honest, open, and credible. Integrity is critical to our credibility."

Huhn's team of negotiators uses a well-structured process designed to make sure that the philosophy of integrity is pervasive throughout the negotiation and not just a function of who happens to be at the table on any given day. It begins with the formation of a negotiation team. Because transition in complex outsourcing transactions represents a period of high vulnerability, it is important to involve implementation staff early on; that way, any commitments made can be validated by those who will be responsible for keeping them. A typical negotiation team consists of a business leader, or pursuit lead, who is usually responsible for developing the business and structuring the transaction; a contract specialist, who brings experience with outsourcing

---

Improving the implementability of deals is not just about layering controls or capturing data. After all, a manager's strength has much to do with the skills she chooses to build and reward and the example she sets with her own questions and actions. In the health care arena, where payer-provider contentions are legion, forward-thinking payers and innovative providers are among those trying to change the dynamics of deals and develop agreements that work better. Blue Cross and Blue Shield of Florida, for example, has been working to institutionalize an approach to payer-provider negotiations that strengthens the working relationship and supports implementation. Training in collaborative negotiation tools and techniques has been rolled down from the senior executives to the negotiators to the support and analysis teams. Even more

contract terms and conditions; and the proposed client manager, who will be responsible for delivery.

Negotiation leads work with a high degree of autonomy. Huhn believes that a negotiator without authority is little more than a messenger, and messengers are unlikely to earn trust or build working relationships with counterparts. At HP, negotiators earn that autonomy by preparing extensively with templates and by reviewing key deal parameters with management. A negotiator's mandate does not just cover price: It also encompasses margins, cash flow, and ROI at different times in the life of the contract; the treatment of transferred employees; the ways various kinds of risk will be allocated; and how the relationship will be governed. All these interests must be addressed—both in preparation and at the negotiation table.

HP's outsourcing negotiators are subject to informal reviews with full-time deal coaches as well as formal milestone reviews. The reviews, which are designed to get key stakeholders committed to implementation, happen before the formal proposal is delivered and before the deal is signed.

The pursuit team leaders aren't finished once the agreement is signed. In fact, they retain responsibility during the transition phase and are considered "liable" for the deal's performance during the next 18 to 24 months. That means negotiators can't simply jump to the next alluring deal. On the contrary, they have a vested interest in making sure the closed deal actually meets its targets.

important, those who manage relationships with providers and are responsible for implementing the agreements are given the same training and tools. In other words, the entire process of putting the deal together, making it work, and feeding the lessons learned through implementation back into the negotiation process has been tightly integrated.

Most competitive runners will tell you that if you train to get to the finish line, you will lose the race. To win, you have to envision your goal as just beyond the finish line so you will blow right past it at full speed. The same is true for a negotiator: If signing the document is your ultimate goal, you will fall short of a winning deal.

The product of a negotiation isn't a document; it's the value produced once the parties have done what they agreed to do. Negotiators who understand that prepare differently than deal makers do. They don't ask, "What might they be willing to accept?" but rather, "How do we create value together?" They also negotiate differently, recognizing that value comes not from a signature but from real work performed long after the ink has dried.

Originally published in November 2004. Reprint R0411C

Notes

1. For more perspectives on Concert's demise, see Margie Semilof's 2001 article "Concert Plays Its Last Note" on InternetWeek.com; Brian Washburn's 2000 article "Disconcerted" on Tele.com; and Charles Hodson's 2001 article "Concert: What Went Wrong?" on CNN.com.

2. See Alec Klein, "Lord of the Flies," the *Washington Post*, June 15, 2003, and Gary Rivlin, "AOL's Rough Riders," *Industry Standard*, October 30, 2000, for more information on the AOL Business Affairs Department's practices.

When to Walk Away from a Deal

by Geoffrey Cullinan, Jean-Marc Le Roux, and Rolf-Magnus Weddigen

DEAL MAKING IS GLAMOROUS; due diligence is not. That simple statement goes a long way toward explaining why so many companies have made so many acquisitions that have produced so little value. Although big companies often make a show of carefully analyzing the size and scope of a deal in question—assembling large teams and spending pots of money—the fact is, the momentum of the transaction is hard to resist once senior management has the target in its sights. Due diligence all too often becomes an exercise in verifying the target's financial statements rather than conducting a fair analysis of the deal's strategic logic and the acquirer's ability to realize value from it. Seldom does the process lead managers to kill potential acquisitions, even when the deals are deeply flawed.

Take the case of Safeway, a leading American grocery chain with a string of successful mergers to its credit and a highly respected management team. In 1998, Safeway acquired Dominick's, an innovative regional grocer in the Chicago area. The strategic logic for the $1.8 billion deal seemed impeccable. It would add about 11% to Safeway's overall sales at a time when mass retailers like Wal-Mart and Kmart were stocking groceries on their shelves and taking market share away from established players, and it would give Safeway a strong presence in a major metropolitan market. Although

Dominick's 7.5% operating cash flow margin lagged behind Safeway's 8.4%, Safeway CEO Steve Burd convinced investors that he would be able to quickly raise the acquired firm's margin to 9.5%. Capitalizing on this momentum, Safeway closed the deal in just five weeks, about a third of the average closing period for large acquisitions.

Safeway would come to regret not taking time for due diligence. Dominick's focus on prepared foods, in-store cafés, and product variety did not fit Safeway's emphasis on store brands and cost discipline. Dominick's strong unions resisted Safeway's aggressive cost-cutting plans. And with its customers unwilling to accept Safeway's private label goods, Dominick's was soon losing share to its archrival, Jewel. A thorough due diligence process would certainly have revealed these problems, and Safeway could have walked away with its pockets intact. Instead, it is stuck with an operation it cannot sell for even a fifth of the original purchase price.

Safeway is just one of many companies to suffer from weak due diligence. In December 2002, Bain & Company surveyed 250 international executives with M&A responsibilities. Half the participants said their due diligence processes had failed to uncover major problems, and half found that their targets had been dressed up to look better for the deals. Two-thirds said they routinely overestimated the synergies available from their acquisitions. Overall, only 30% of the executives were satisfied with the rigor of their due diligence processes. Fully a third admitted they hadn't walked away from deals they had nagging doubts about.

What can companies do to improve their due diligence? To answer that question, we've taken a close look at 20 companies—both public and private—whose transactions have demonstrated high-quality due diligence. We calibrated our findings against our experiences in 2,000-odd deals we've screened over the past 10 years. We've found that successful acquirers view due diligence as much more than an exercise in verifying data. While they go through the numbers deeply and thoroughly, they also put the broader, strategic rationale for their acquisitions under the microscope. They look at the business case in its entirety, probing for strengths and weaknesses and searching for unreliable assumptions and other

Idea in Brief

Is your company prone to "deal fever"—getting so excited while pursuing acquisitions that it skimps on due diligence? Caught up in the thrill of the chase, many firms use due diligence to justify the deal rather than to uncover potentially serious problems.

To introduce discipline into your due diligence, Cullinan, Le Roux, and Weddigen recommend putting potential acquisitions' strategic rationale under the microscope: Probe for targets' strengths and weaknesses, and dig for unreliable assumptions. Be prepared to walk away.

Asking four questions can protect your company from ending up with a bad bargain:

- What are we *really* buying? (What would the acquisition bring, in terms of customers, competitors, costs, and capabilities?)

- What's the target's stand-alone value? (Your purchase price should reflect the target as it is, not as it might be once acquired.)

- Where are the synergies?

- What's the most we're willing to pay?

flaws in the logic. They take a highly disciplined and objective approach to the process, and their senior executives pay close heed to the results of the investigations and analyses—to the extent that they are prepared to walk away from a deal, even in the very late stages of negotiations. For these companies, due diligence acts as a counter-weight to the excitement that builds when managers begin to pursue a target.

The successful acquirers we studied were all consistent in their approach to due diligence. Although there were idiosyncrasies and differences in emphasis placed on their inquiries, all of them built their due diligence process as an investigation into four basic questions:

- What are we *really* buying?

- What is the target's stand-alone value?

- Where are the synergies—and the skeletons?

- What's our walk-away price?

Idea in Practice

Cullinan, Le Roux, and Weddigen offer these guidelines for evaluating a potential acquisition:

What Are We *Really* Buying?

Instead of relying on information provided by the target company, build your own view of the target by gathering information on its:

- **Customers:** Who are the target's most profitable customers, and how well is it managing them? For example, how do its customers' profitability or vulnerability compare with those of the target's competitors?

- **Competition:** How does the target compare to rivals in terms of market share, revenues, and profits—by geography, product, and segment? How might its competitors react to the acquisition?

- **Costs:** Is the target performing above or below cost expectations given its relative market position? Why? What's the best cost position you could reasonably achieve by acquiring the target?

- **Capabilities:** What capabilities—management expertise, technologies, organizational structures—does the target have that create definable customer value?

What's the Target's Stand-Alone Value?

The vast majority of the price you pay for an acquisition should reflect the business as it is, not as it might be once you've won it. To determine stand-alone value, strip away tricks used by targets, such as stuffing distribution channels to inflate sales projections.

In the following pages, we'll examine each of these questions in depth, demonstrating how they can provide any company with a solid framework for effective due diligence.

What Are We *Really* Buying?

When senior executives begin to look at an acquisition, they quickly develop a mental image of the target company, often drawing on its public profile or its reputation within the business community. That mental image shapes the entire deal-making process—it turns into the story that management tells itself about the deal. An effective due diligence process challenges this mental model, getting at the real story beneath the often heavily varnished surface. Rather

Send a team into the field to see what's really happening with the target's costs and sales. If the target's hesitant or hostile about your investigation, steer clear.

Where Are the Synergies—and Dangers?

Assess the value of the acquisition's potential cost and revenue synergies by:

- **Estimating how long they'll take to achieve.** You can gain some synergies (such as eliminating duplicate functions) quickly. Others (such as selling new products through new channels) take much longer.

- **Assessing the probability of success.** Some synergies (such as combining facilities) have lower success rates because they involve complex personnel and regulatory issues.

- **Considering integration costs.** Anticipate post-acquisition events that can sap revenues or increase costs, such as defections of talented employees.

What's Our Walk-Away Price?

Your walk-away price is the top price you're willing to pay when the final negotiation is conducted. When establishing your walk-away price, give most weight to the current worth of the target company, and don't overestimate synergies' potential value—which may not materialize. Assemble a team of trusted individuals, less attached to the deal than senior management, who can provide an unbiased examination of the target and hold everyone to the walk-away criteria.

than rely on secondary sources and biased forecasts provided by the target company itself, the corporate suitor must build its own proprietary, bottom-up view of the target and its industry, gathering information about customers, suppliers, and competitors in the field.

Bridgepoint, a leading European private equity firm, is particularly adept at this kind of strategic due diligence. In 2000, Bridgepoint was considering buying a fruit-processing business from the French liquor giant Pernod Ricard. The business, which for the purposes of this article we'll call FruitCo, looked like an attractive acquisition candidate. As the leading producer of the fruit mixtures used to flavor yogurt, it was well positioned in a growing industry. Western consumers had been spending between 5% and 10% more each year on yogurt, and the market was growing faster still in the developing world, particularly in Latin America and Asia. FruitCo was posting profits and had won praise for its innovativeness and its excellence in R&D and manufacturing. Moreover, there was nothing suspicious about Pernod Ricard's reasons for selling—fruit processing simply lay outside its core business.

FruitCo looked like a winner to Benoît Bassi, a managing director of Bridgepoint in Paris. He saw attractive opportunities to boost FruitCo's revenues and profits by expanding the business into adjacent categories, such as ice cream and baked goods, as well as into new channels. After laying out the case for the acquisition in a grueling five-hour meeting with his partners, Bassi got the OK to pursue the deal. Yet it never happened; just four weeks later, Bassi killed it.

During those four weeks, the due diligence team had discovered many worms in the shiny FruitCo apple. They tested the argument that FruitCo could make money by scaling up and competing on cost, for instance. And they found that while the company boasted considerable global scale, regional scale turned out to be the more relevant driver of costs. That was because the economics of transportation and purchasing made the global sourcing of fruit—a major cost component—unfeasible. At the same time, advanced processing technologies enabled FruitCo's rivals to achieve competitive economics at the country level. When the team tested FruitCo's price and revenue forecasts, they found further cause for concern. The market for fruit yogurt was indeed growing, but profitability in many markets—particularly in Latin America—was falling rapidly, indicating that the product was turning into a commodity. Stemming this trend seemed unlikely; consumers told Bridgepoint's researchers that they would be unlikely to tolerate increased prices. The team then pored over the target company's customer lists. They found that FruitCo was highly dependent on sales to two large yogurt producers, both of which seemed intent on achieving more control over the entire production process in each major market that they competed in. FruitCo seemed fated to an erosion of market power—it would have to fight for every contract.

Bassi recognized that the original business case for the acquisition did not hold up under close scrutiny. He walked away from the deal he had once coveted, probably saving Bridgepoint millions of dollars in the process. "What we thought we knew turned out to be wrong," Bassi unsentimentally explains.

As the story suggests, effective acquirers systematically test a deal's strategic logic. Like Bridgepoint, they typically organize their investigations around the four Cs of competition: customers, competitors, costs, and capabilities (often but not necessarily in that order). Within each of these areas, due diligence teams ask hard questions as they study their targets. Although they will rely on information provided by the targets, they do not accept those data at face value. They conduct their own field analyses.

Get to know the customers

Good due diligence practitioners begin by drawing a map of their target's market, sketching out its size, its growth rate, and how it breaks down by geography, product, and customer segment. This allows them to compare the target's customer segments—their profitability, promise, and vulnerability—with those of its competitors. Has the target fully penetrated some customer segments but neglected others? What is the target's track record in retaining customers? Where could you adjust its offerings to grow sales or increase prices? What channels does the target use to serve its customers, and how do those channels match your own? In researching these questions, effective due diligence teams remember always to identify the target's most profitable customers and look at how well the target is managing them. They don't rely on what the target tells them about its customers; they approach the customers directly.

Check out the competition

Good due diligence practitioners always examine the target's industry presence—How does it compare to its rivals in terms of market share, revenues, and profits by geography, product, and segment? They look at the pool of available profits and try to determine whether the target is getting a fair (or better) share of industry profits compared with its rivals. How does each competitor make the profits expected from a company with its relative market share? Where in the value chain are profits concentrated? Is there a way to capture more? Is the target underperforming operationally? Are its competitors? Is the business correctly defined? The due diligence team should carefully consider how competitors will react to the acquisition and how that might affect the business. Once again, effective teams don't rely on what the target tells them; they seek independent advice.

Verify the cost economics

Successful due diligence teams always ask the following questions about costs: Do the target's competitors have cost advantages? Why is the target performing above or below expectations given its relative market position? What is the best cost position the acquirer could reasonably achieve? The team also needs to look at the extent to which the target is using its experience in the market to drive down costs. When considering postmerger opportunities for cost rationalization, the team needs to assess whether the benefit of sharing costs with other business units will outweigh the lack of focus that sharing costs across multiple businesses might introduce. It needs to determine how low it can take costs by instituting best practices. Benchmarking can be an important aid here. It's also vital to look at how to allocate costs going forward. Which products and customers really make the money, and which ones should be dropped?

Take stock of capabilities

Effective acquirers always remember that they are not just buying a P&L and a balance sheet but also capabilities such as management expertise. Capabilities may not be easy to measure, but taking them for granted is too large a risk for any company because competencies largely determine how well a company will be able to pursue its postacquisition strategy. Acquirers should ask themselves: What special skills or technologies does the target have that create definable customer value? How can it leverage those core competencies? What investments in technology and people will help buttress the existing competencies? What competencies can the company do without? Assessing capabilities also involves looking at which organizational structures will enable the business to implement its strategy most effectively. How should all other aspects of the organization (such as compensation, incentives, promotion, information flow, authority, and autonomy) be aligned with the strategy?

In testing a deal's strategic logic, most companies will be on the lookout for potential problems—the smoking guns, the skeletons in the closets. But the due diligence process can produce nice surprises as easily as nasty ones, and it may give a would-be acquirer a reason to pursue a deal more aggressively than it otherwise might have. Centre Partners' acquisition in the late 1990s of American Seafoods, a fishing company, is a case in point. (See the sidebar "Uncovering Hidden Treasure.")

What Is the Target's Stand-Alone Value?

Once the wheels of an acquisition are turning, it becomes difficult for senior managers to step on the brakes; they become too invested in the deal's success. Here, again, due diligence should play a critical role by imposing objective discipline on the financial side of the process. What you find in your bottom-up assessment of the target and its industry must translate into concrete benefits in revenue, cost and earnings, and, ultimately, cash flow. At the same time, the target's books should be rigorously analyzed not just to verify reported numbers and assumptions but also to determine the business's true value as a stand-alone concern. The vast majority of the price you pay reflects the business as is, not as it might be once you've won it. Too often the reverse is true: The fundamentals of the business for sale are unattractive relative to its price, so the search begins for synergies to justify the deal.

Of course, determining a company's true value is easier said than done. Ever since the old days of the barter economy, when farmers would exaggerate the health and understate the age of the livestock they were trading, sellers have always tried to dress up their assets to make them look more appealing than they really are. That's certainly true in business today, when companies can use a wide

Uncovering Hidden Treasure

A COMPREHENSIVE DUE DILIGENCE EFFORT can uncover good news as well as bad. In some cases, it can even lead a company to make a strong acquisition that it might otherwise have passed up. That's what happened when the private equity firm Centre Partners looked into buying a fishing company called American Seafoods in the late 1990s. The company caught and processed Alaskan pollock and other species from seven fishing trawlers operating in U.S. waters in the Bering Sea. At the time, American Seafoods was owned by a Norwegian parent company. But when the U.S. Congress enacted a law that made it illegal for a foreign concern to own companies fishing in American waters, the Norwegian parent was forced to sell.

Although American Seafoods' profits jumped in 1999—its EBITDA hit $60 million that year, more than double the annual average of approximately $26 million in the three preceding years—the fishing business did not, at first blush, seem particularly attractive to Centre Partners. Historically subject to wide swings in supplies and prices and under increasingly tight regulation, the business seemed fated to volatile and potentially weak returns. But when Centre Partners sent in a crack due diligence team, combining experts in consumer products, fishing operations, and marine biology, it found that, far from being a blip, American Seafoods' profit boom appeared sustainable.

The team's global analysis of the health of major fisheries turned up the most interesting data. Centre Partners discovered that the total biomass of

range of accounting tricks to buff their numbers. Here are just a few of the most common examples of financial trickery used:

- **Stuffing distribution channels to inflate sales projections.**
  For instance, a company may treat as market sales many of the products it sells to distributors—which may not represent recurring sales.

- **Using overoptimistic projections to inflate the expected returns from investments in new technologies and other capital expenditures.** A company might, for example, assume that a major uptick in its cross selling will enable it to recoup its large investment in customer relationship management software.

- **Disguising the head count of cost centers by decentralizing functions so you never see the full picture.** For instance,

the U.S. Alaskan pollock fishery was expected to grow in coming years, while the biomasses of competing fisheries—Russian Alaskan pollock and Atlantic cod, most notably—were dropping, some at a fast clip. Overall supplies of pollock and cod would fall, in other words, but the share of the market represented by U.S. Alaskan pollock would probably rise. That was good news from a revenue and pricing standpoint, and the news got even better when the due diligence team looked more closely at trends in fish prices. Although pollock prices had recently increased, as overall supplies fell, they remained well below the levels of competing whitefish like cod, tilapia, and hoki. As a result, there seemed little chance that pollock would be subject to significant price competition for the foreseeable future. The big Japanese market for pollock roe, meanwhile, remained strong while supplies were falling, leading to a sharp and sustainable increase in roe prices that seemed likely to benefit American Seafoods well into the future.

Based on the results of the due diligence analysis, Centre Partners made a successful bid for American Seafoods. It turned out to be quite a catch. Within three years, EBITDA grew to $109 million, and the private equity firm had recapitalized the company and sold a portion of its stake. Today, the firm is exploring an initial public offering. In the process, Centre Partners realized nearly four times its initial investment and retained control of the business as it sought to further grow revenue and increase profits.

some companies scatter the marketing function among field offices and maintain just a coordinating crew at headquarters, which hides the true overhead.

- **Treating recurring items as extraordinary costs to get them off the P&L.** A company might, for example, use the restructuring of a sales network as a way to declare bad receivables as a onetime expense.

- **Exaggerating a website's potential for being an effective, cheap sales channel.**

- **Underfunding capital expenditures or sales, general, and administrative costs in the periods leading up to a sale to make cash flow look healthier.** For example, a manufacturer may decide to postpone its machine renewals a year or two so those figures won't be immediately visible in the books. But the manufacturer will overstate free cash flow—and possibly mislead the investor about how much regular capital a plant needs.

- **Encouraging the sales force to boost sales while hiding costs.** A company looking for a buyer might, for example, offer advantageous terms and conditions on postsale service to boost current sales. The product revenues will show up immediately in the P&L, but the lower profit margin on service revenues will not be apparent until much later.

To arrive at a business's true stand-alone value, all these accounting tricks must be stripped away to reveal the historical and prospective cash flows. Often, the only way to do this is to look beyond the reported numbers—to send a due diligence team into the field to see what's really happening with costs and sales.

That's what Cinven, a leading European private equity company, did before acquiring Odeon Cinemas, a UK theater chain, in 2000. Instead of looking at the aggregate revenues and costs, as Odeon reported them, Cinven's analysts combed through the numbers of every individual cinema in order to understand the P&L dynamics at each location. They were able to paint a rich picture of local demand patterns and competitor activities, including data on attendance, revenues, operating costs, and capital expenditures that would be required over the next five years. This microexamination of the company revealed that the initial market valuation was flawed; estimates of sales growth at the national level were not justified by local trends. Armed with the findings, Cinven negotiated to pay £45 million less than the original asking price.

Getting ground-level numbers usually requires the close cooperation of the acquisition target's top brass. An adversarial posture almost always backfires. Cinven, for example, took pains to explain to Odeon's executives that a deep understanding of Odeon's business would help ensure the ultimate success of the merger. Cinven and Odeon executives worked as a team to examine the results of each cinema and to test the assumptions of Odeon's business model. They held four daylong meetings in which they went through each of the sites and agreed on the most important levers for revenue and profit growth in the local markets. Although the process may strike the target company as excessively intrusive, target managers will find there are a number of benefits to going along with it beyond pleasing a potential acquirer. Even if the deal with Cinven had fallen apart, Odeon would have emerged from the deal's due diligence process with a much better understanding of its own economics.

Of course, no matter how friendly the approach, many targets will be prickly. The company may have something to hide. Or the target's managers may just want to retain their independence; people who believe that knowledge is power naturally like to hold on to that knowledge. But innocent or not, a target's hesitancy or outright hostility during due diligence is a sign that a deal's value will be more difficult to realize than originally expected. As Joe Trustey, managing partner of private equity firm Summit Partners, says: "We walk away from a target whose management is uncooperative in due diligence. For us, that's a deal breaker."

Where Are the Synergies—and the Skeletons?

It's hard to be realistic about the synergies an acquisition will deliver. In the fevered environment of a takeover, managers routinely overestimate the value of cost and revenue synergies and underestimate the difficulty of achieving them. It's worth repeating that two-thirds of the executives in our M&A survey admitted to having overestimated the synergies available from combining companies.

Realizing that synergy estimates are often untrustworthy, some companies have made it their policy not to take potential synergies into account when determining the value of acquisition candidates. Although the concern behind the policy is understandable, such an approach can be destructive: Some synergies are achievable, and ignoring them may steer companies away from smart acquisitions. A better approach is to use the due diligence process to carefully distinguish between different kinds of synergies, and then estimate both their potential value and the probability that they can be realized. That assessment should also include the speed with which the synergies can be achieved and the investments it will take to get them.

We've found it useful to think of potential synergies as a series of concentric circles, as shown in the exhibit "A map of synergies." The synergies at the center come from eliminating duplicate functions, business activities, and costs—for instance, combining legal staffs, treasury oversight, and board expenses. These are the easiest synergies to achieve; companies are sure to realize most of the potential savings here. The next closest circle represents the savings realized from cutting shared operating costs, such as distribution, sales, and regional overhead expenses. Most companies will realize the majority of these savings, as well. Then come the savings from facilities rationalization, which are typically more difficult to achieve because they can involve significant personnel and regulatory issues. Farther out are the more elusive revenue synergies, starting with sales of existing products through new channels and moving to the outermost circle, selling new products through new channels. Each circle offers large rewards, but the farther out the savings or revenues lie, the more difficult they become to achieve and the longer it will take. Categorizing synergies in this way provides a useful framework for valuing them. Analysts can assign to each circle a potential value, a probability for achieving the value, and a timetable for implementation, which can be used to model the synergies' effect on the combined cash flows of the companies.

It's important that this analysis also explicitly consider the cost of achieving the synergies, in both cash and time. In one dramatic case, the Canadian real estate companies O&Y Properties and Bentall Capital called off their planned merger in 2003 after tallying up the integration costs necessary to realize the synergies. O&Y managed properties throughout eastern Canada, while Bentall's holdings were concentrated in the West. In addition to complementing each other geographically, the two companies believed they could rationalize expenses over a larger collection of properties and still have representatives on the ground in every major North American city. Yet, after due diligence, both sides realized that the high costs

A map of synergies

A deal's potential synergies are best viewed as a series of concentric circles. Those close to the center tend to be cost-saving synergies, which can be realized quickly and are likely to succeed. Those on the outside are revenue-generating synergies, which require a lot of time and management and are less likely to succeed. In determining your walk-away price, your discount factor for synergies should rise as you move away from the center.

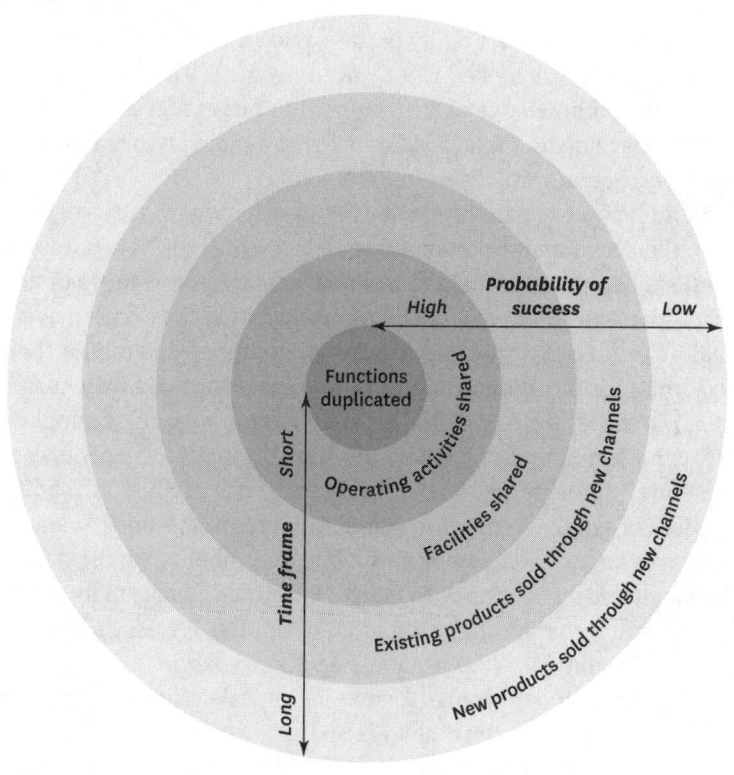

of integration would likely overwhelm any long-run savings and revenue gains. Bentall president Gary Whitelaw told the press that his company had grown "increasingly concerned that the scale of the integration could divert resources away from our primary objective. . . . The merger risks would have been significant, demanding increased management attention, and resulting in larger integration costs than at first may have been thought." The deal was scuttled, to the benefit of O&Y's and Bentall's shareholders.

It is perhaps understandable that managers might want to put off thinking about the sensitive issues inherent in integration planning until after the deal is signed and sealed. But that is often a serious mistake. Integration planning—and the costs of integration—are among the biggest determinants of an acquisition's ultimate success or failure, and you can't really declare a due diligence process complete unless you've looked closely at those costs. The due diligence team's deep knowledge of the acquisition target makes it an ideal body to develop an initial road map for combining two companies' staffs and operations.

In addition to examining the cost of achieving positive synergies, the due diligence team also needs to consider how potential conflicts between the merged businesses may sap revenues or add costs. These negative synergies—the skeletons in the closet of every deal—can take many forms. Once two companies combine their accounts, for example, some of their joint customers may curtail their purchases for fear of being overly reliant on a single supplier. Difficulties in integrating back-office operations or systems may at least briefly impede customer service and order fulfillment, leading to a loss of sales. Seeing more competition for promotions, talented employees may leave, sometimes taking customers with them. And the inevitable distractions of a merger may force management to pay less attention to the core business, undermining its results. Despite their often immense importance, negative synergies are routinely overlooked in due diligence. A common mistake, for example, is to create a valuation model that adds up the revenues of the two companies, plus the synergies, without subtracting an estimated amount for revenue erosion or increased costs.

Even the best acquirers will encounter negative synergies. An executive who left cereal giant Kellogg after its 2001 merger with biscuit maker Keebler told us that the company experienced negative synergies when it decided to put new-product launches on hold in order to focus on integrating the two companies. Some potential revenues were lost as a result even though Kellogg met its targets for cost reductions. A more devastating example of negative synergies occurred in the 1996 merger of the Southern Pacific and the Union Pacific railroads. Incompatibilities in the companies' information systems, combined with other operating conflicts, created massive disruptions in rail traffic throughout the western United States, leading to delayed and misrouted shipments and irate customers. In the end, the government had to declare a federal transportation emergency.

What's Our Walk-Away Price?

The final leg of a sound due diligence process is determining a walk-away price—the top price you are willing to pay when the final price negotiation is conducted.

The walk-away price should never include the full potential value of the synergies, which is why it's important to calculate the deal's stand-alone value separately. Synergies—especially the elusive outer-circle synergies—are something that you target in managing a completed acquisition; they should not unduly influence the negotiation of the deal unless you can be fairly certain about the numbers.

For a walk-away price to have meaning, you really have to be willing to walk away. A useful lesson in that regard comes from Kellogg's CEO, Carlos Gutierrez, who negotiated the purchase of Keebler. Gutierrez dearly wanted to close the deal. Keebler's vaunted direct-to-store delivery system enabled it to carry products to stores in its own trucks, bypassing the retailers' warehouses altogether. Gutierrez saw enormous potential for funneling Kellogg products through Keebler's highly efficient system. But Kellogg's rigorous due diligence analysis made it clear that the maximum he should pay for Keebler was $42 a share, which he expected was less than what Keebler was looking for. "Even though this was a deal that we desperately wanted," Gutierrez later recalled, "I conditioned myself mentally to say we might not have it." In a final bargaining session in New York, Gutierrez told Keebler's management that a share price of $42 was his maximum offer—and that if they could get more from someone else, they should take it. Gutierrez went off to watch a Mets game, determined not to give any more thought to the negotiation. Two days later, Keebler accepted Gutierrez's offer.

To establish a walk-away price, successful deal makers convene a decision-making body of trusted individuals who are less attached to the deal than senior management is. They insist on senior management's approval of the body and establish a decision-making process that clearly delineates who in the company recommends deals, who holds veto power, whose input should be solicited, and who decides yea or nay in the final instance. They adopt formal checks and balances that rely on predetermined walk-away criteria.

Bridgepoint assembles a team of six managers, each of whom represents one of four viewpoints. One is the prosecutor, who plays the role of devil's advocate. The second is the less-experienced manager, whose involvement is a key part of his or her training. The third is a senior managing director, who no longer has any hierarchical function at the company and who therefore cannot be undermined by corporate politics. The final members of the panel are managing directors who still have operational roles. The team's goal is to provide a thorough, balanced, and unbiased examination of the acquisition candidate and hold everyone's feet to the fire on walk-away criteria. "That makes quite a balanced whole," says Bridgepoint's Bassi. "Is it perfect? I don't know. But it works."

Companies can also adjust their compensation systems as added incentive against overpaying for deals. For instance, at Clear Channel, an international radio, billboard, and live entertainment company, line managers have to sign off "in blood," as CFO Randall Mays puts it, on the cash flows that any acquisitions will deliver. The company ties managers' future compensation to meeting the division's cash flow projections, which include results from those acquisitions. The salaries for Clear Channel's M&A teams are also tied to the contribution that acquisitions make to the company's financial performance. The division presidents and M&A teams meet Mays at year's end to study all the acquisitions they have made in the previous three years to see whether they delivered what they promised and to review compensation at the same time. As Mays puts it, the deals they make "are tied to them forever."

———————

The backward-looking science of due diligence is vital. But it is a meaningless exercise without the forward-looking art of *strategic* due diligence. In the wake of so many disappointing mergers and acquisitions, more and more organizations are realizing that there are few better ways of spending managers' time and investors' money than in a careful and creative analysis of an acquisition candidate.

In the end, effective due diligence is as much about managerial humility as anything else. It's about testing every assumption and questioning every belief. It's about not falling into the trap of thinking you'll be able to fix any problem after the fact. The best private equity firms are particularly good models in this regard, since they look at every potential deal coldly, without bias or overconfidence. As Bridgepoint's Benoît Bassi puts it, "When you work for a corporation and you buy something you think is in your core business or fits with your core business, you assume you know what you are buying. By contrast, [private equity investors] have to rediscover everything. There can be a certain arrogance in corporations, which causes them to make silly mistakes." And those silly mistakes can end up costing companies millions, or even billions, of dollars.

Originally published in April 2004. Reprint R0404F

MAX H. BAZERMAN is the Jesse Isidor Straus Professor of Business Administration at Harvard Business School and a codirector of the Center for Public Leadership at Harvard Kennedy School.

ALISON WOOD BROOKS is an assistant professor at Harvard Business School. She teaches negotiation in the MBA and executive education curricula and is affiliated with the Behavioral Insights Group.

DIANE L. COUTU is the director of client communications at Banyan Family Business Advisors, headquartered in Cambridge, Massachusetts, and the author of the HBR article "How Resilience Works."

GEOFFREY CULLINAN is a partner and adviser at Bain & Company. He founded and led Bain's private equity business.

DANNY ERTEL is a founder and director of Vantage Partners, a consulting firm in Boston, and CEO and chairman of Vantage Technologies, which develops software to enable negotiation and relationship management processes.

DANIEL KAHNEMAN is professor of psychology and public affairs emeritus at the Woodrow Wilson School and the Eugene Higgins Professor of Psychology Emeritus at Princeton University.

DEBORAH M. KOLB is professor of management at the Simmons College Graduate School of Management in Boston and codirector of its Center for Gender in Organizations. She is a former executive director of the Program on Negotiation at Harvard Law School, where she continues as codirector of the Negotiations in the Workplace Project.

DAVID A. LAX is the managing principal at Lax Sebenius, a negotiation strategy firm.

JEAN-MARC LE ROUX is a partner and director at Bain & Company, where he leads their private equity practice in France.

DEEPAK MALHOTRA is the Eli Goldston Professor of Business Administration at Harvard Business School and the author of *Negotiating the Impossible* (Berrett-Koehler, 2016).

ERIN MEYER is a professor and the program director for Managing Global Virtual Teams at INSEAD. She is the author of *The Culture Map: Breaking Through the Invisible Boundaries of Global Business* (PublicAffairs, 2014).

JAMES K. SEBENIUS is the Gordon Donaldson Professor of Business Administration at Harvard Business School, director of the Harvard Negotiation Project based at Harvard Law School, and chair of the Great Negotiator Program at the Program on Negotiation.

ROLF-MAGNUS WEDDIGEN is a partner at Bain & Company, where he leads the firm's German and Swiss private equity practice.

JUDITH WILLIAMS, a former investment banker, is the founder of Anagram, a nonprofit corporation in Boston dedicated to the study of social and organizational change.

Index

The most important management ideas all in one place.

We hope you enjoyed this book from *Harvard Business Review*. Now you can get even more with HBR's 10 Must Reads Boxed Set. From books on leadership and strategy to managing yourself and others, this 6-book collection delivers articles on the most essential business topics to help you succeed.

HBR's 10 Must Reads Series

The definitive collection of ideas and best practices on our most sought-after topics from the best minds in business.

- Change Management
- Collaboration
- Communication
- Emotional Intelligence
- Innovation
- Leadership
- Making Smart Decisions

- Managing Across Cultures
- Managing People
- Managing Yourself
- Strategic Marketing
- Strategy
- Teams
- The Essentials

hbr.org/mustreads